YOU CAN TEACH YOURSELF™

SONG WRITING

WITHDRAWN

by
Larry
McCabe

A cassette tape of the music in this
book is now available. The publisher
strongly recommends the use of this
cassette tape along with the text to
insure accuracy of interpretation and
ease in learning.

CONTENTS

INTRODUCTION

Welcome to the exciting world of songwriting! This book is for anyone who wants to learn the fundamental techniques used by professional song writers. Whether you are a student, a hobbyist, or one who aspires to a songwriting career, these lessons will help you improve your songwriting in your own style, and at your own pace.

I suggest that you begin with Chapter One (Getting Started), which will help you set goals and get organized. After that, you may study the lessons in any order you choose. Do you want to study the twelve-bar blues form? Turn to Chapter Two. Are you interested in the basics of Copyright law? Read Chapter Eight. Maybe you wish to learn how to create a melody; if so, see Chapter Four. Look up each subject according to your interests and needs, and soon you will develop a well-rounded, comprehensive approach to writing songs.

No matter what style of songwriting you are interested in, you will find a wealth of information here, all presented in an easy-to-use format, and explained in easy-to-understand language. For sheer pleasure, few activities can match songwriting, and I wish you the best of success as you apply these lessons to your original creations.

Larry McCabe
Tallahassee, Florida

1

GETTING STARTED

Chapter One offers helpful guidelines for getting organized and establishing your song-writing goals. After reading this introductory material, you may work through the remaining chapters in any order you choose.

WHAT ASPECTS OF SONGWRITING CAN BE TAUGHT AND LEARNED?

Almost all new songwriters are curious to know to what extent songwriting can actually be taught. The first prerequisite to successful songwriting is to have the intuitive desire to learn the craft. Learning any craft means acquiring the skills that have been mastered by the professionals. By studying educational materials such as this book, the aspiring songwriter can learn many essential songwriting skills such as:

1. Song form
2. Methods for writing lyrics
3. How to create a melody
4. How to create chord progressions
5. How to understand the relationship between melody and chords
6. Rhythms
7. How to use music theory as a shortcut to good results
8. The realities of the commercial songwriting business
9. How to look for ideas and inspiration
10. How to get organized and focus on important objectives

In addition to the above, a qualified teacher can provide encouragement, guidance, answer questions, give valuable feedback, and expose the student to a broad range of musical styles.

Skills that cannot actually be taught are: 1) inspiration, 2) originality, 3) feelings, 4) imagination, and 5) spontaneity. These qualities cannot be induced, and must come from within.

SIXTEEN TIPS FOR THE ASPIRING SONGWRITER

1. **Enjoy your work**. Relax and enjoy the process of writing songs. If it is a continual struggle, it is not the right work for you.
2. **Think positive**. Always think "I can."
3. **Set realistic goals**. Plan ahead, perhaps in 3-month blocks of time.
4. **Be dedicated and consistent**. Dedicate as much of yourself as possible to songwriting, and write as often as possible.
5. **Focus** by eliminating outside distractions. Seek solitude and exercise self-discipline.
6. **Develop your skills** consistently by studying, analyzing, and practicing. Learn to be a problem solver, and keep yourself "tuned up" and up-to-date.
7. **Learn to evaluate criticism**. All artistic work is subject to criticism. When your work is criticized, try to make an honest judgment as to whether or not the criticism is valid.
8. **Learn to accept meaningful criticism**. Honest feedback from professionals is one of the greatest of all learning experiences. All creative people must be willing to accept criticism and respond to it in a constructive manner.
9. **Be original**. There is only one Bob Dylan, one Paul Simon, and one *you*.

10. **Be open-minded about music**. Expose yourself to a broad range of musical styles.

11. **Be patient**. Success rarely occurs overnight, but it often occurs as a result of determination and self-confidence.

12. **Be persistent**. Persevere – don't give up easily.

13. **Set high standards for yourself**. Why settle for work of inferior quality? Review, rewrite, consolidate and double-check.

14. **Be honest with yourself**. If something is not working, try another way.

15. **Expect and accept disappointments**. Occasional disappointment is part of life – why deny it? For the aspiring commercial songwriter, the speculative and competitive nature of the work maximizes the risk of disappointment. Even the great songwriters have experienced letdowns and commercial flops. Often, the ability to withstand disappointments allowed them to develop their skills and become great innovators.

16. **Participate** by joining songwriter societies, attending clinics, entering contests, etc.

HOBBYIST OR PROFESSIONAL?

In regards to songwriting, each individual must ask himself/herself the question: "To what extent do I wish to participate?" Some will view their songwriting efforts as a hobby; others will aspire to professional status.

For the hobbyist, there will be little or no self-induced pressure to meet a deadline, sell a project, or "become famous." Many hobbyists become fairly proficient while deriving consistent satisfaction from their songwriting endeavors. The outlook for the aspiring professional is quite different, for he/she must prepare to compete with creative people who 1) have developed the ability to express themselves in a unique style; 2) are knowledgeable about the business side of songwriting; and 3) have the versatility to respond creatively to many types of work assignments, often on short notice.

CRITERIA FOR EVALUATION OF SONGS

All good songs have one thing in common: an element of originality. Other than that, there is no consensus on exactly what makes a good song. Any song played for a random sample of 100 people will elicit varying opinions as to why the song is good, bad, or mediocre (remember the *American Bandstand* ratings?). Because different listeners have different tastes in music, there are really no exact guidelines for "measuring" the worth of a given tune. For the new songwriter, perhaps the following criteria are a good starting point:

1. Did I enjoy a sense of satisfaction creating this song?

2. Does my song contain elements of originality?

3. Does my song make creative use of the basic elements of music (rhythm, melody, and harmony)?

4. Does my song communicate its intended meaning to my intended audience?

5. Does my audience seem to enjoy and/or understand my song?

THE COMMERCIAL SONGWRITER

The commercial songwriter may be tempted to consolidate the previous questions into three words: "Will it sell?" Therefore, the professional writer must be knowledgeable about changing styles and trends. For instance, country records used to be about truck drivers and honky-tonks. Nowadays, "country" songs touch on such topics as condominiums, the office, and golfing (can you imagine Hank Williams on the golf course?).

THE VALUE OF FUNDAMENTALS

Knowing the fundamentals of music will give you advantages that cannot be overstressed. The ability to manipulate the raw materials of music gives one the advantage of versatility – *and* the ability to efficiently communicate with other musicians.

2

FORM

Repetition and *contrast* are two key elements of good music. The listener who feels comfortable with the familiar is often intrigued by the unexpected. In this chapter, we will study the standard song forms that are widely used in popular music, folk songs, and jazz. These song forms allow the modern composer to achieve a healthy balance between repetition and contrast. A thorough understanding of these compositional formats will greatly enhance your ability to communicate effectively with your listeners. In addition, you will develop a greater understanding of—and appreciation for—the music you listen to every day.

THE AAA SONG FORM

The *AAA song* contains several verses; each verse has the same melody but different words. The AAA song has no chorus or other contrasting melodic sections. Although the term AAA suggests three verses, some AAA songs have many verses. Most AAA songs have lyrics, but a few AAA tunes are instrumentals ("Cantaloupe Island"). Found in all styles, the AAA form is especially prevalent in folk and country. The verses can be any length; however, the 16-bar verse is the most common.

AAA songs usually tell a story that is developed with each successive verse. Because there are no contrasting musical sections, it is very important for the AAA song to contain lyrics that hold the listener's interest. More often than not, the title is placed at the beginning—or at the end—of each verse. The "payoff" or climactic point of the story normally occurs in the final verse—sometimes with a surprise ending.

Examples of AAA tunes include: "Red River Valley," "Wildwood Flower," "Purple Haze," "Bring it on Home to Me," "Yesterdays," and "Early Mornin' Rain."

BARBARA ALLEN

The folk song "Barbara Allen" typifies the AAA or "verse" song form.

Comment/Analysis

Many old English ballads—such as "Barbara Allen"—were written and sung in the AAA style. Typically, these storytelling songs contained many 16-bar verses. Here, I have arranged "Barbara Allen" to fit 14 bars, just to show that we are not restricted to 16.

Recommended Listening

"Barbara Allen," *Joan Baez Vol. 2*, Vanguard VRS 9094-B.

Barbara Allen

Example of Form AAA

In Scar-let town where I was born, there lived a
fair young mai-den. She was the fair - est of them
all, her name was Bar - - 'bry Al - len. ___

Additional verses:

Twas in the merry month of May,
When green buds all were swellin';
Sweet William on his deathbed lay,
For love of Barbara Allen.

He sent his servant to the town,
To the place where she was dwellin';
Sayin' you must come to my master dear,
If your name be Bar'bry Allen.

GUITAR CHORDS

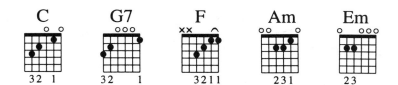

ARRANGING SESSION: AAA

This sketch is a typical example of an AAA tune arranged for performance or recording.

Instrumental Intro.	Verse 1	Verse 2	Instrumental Fill
4 Bars	**16 Bars**	**16 Bars**	**4 Bars**

Verse 3	Instrumental Fill	Verse 4	Vocal Tag	Instrumental End
16 Bars	**4 Bars**	**16 Bars**	**8 Bars**	**4 Bars**

Comment/Analysis

1. A recording of a moderate-tempo AAA song with four (or more) 16-bar verses does not leave much time for solos. This is because of time restrictions on music intended for airplay. Still, it is a good idea to use some instrumental material for variety.

2. Sometimes the final line of lyrics is sung twice (or more) to end the tune. When this technique is used, the repeated line is known as a *tag*.

3. Another way to create a tag is to finish the song by singing only the last half of the last verse.

SONGWRITING PRACTICE
FORM: AAA
LENGTH: 16 BARS

Write an original song by filling in lyrics and/or music on the blank staff.

Tips

1. Write your lyrics (and melody) in four 4-bar phrases.

2. Try to end each phrase by the time you reach the dotted line.

3. Pickup notes may be used to start each phrase.

4. Use the key and time signature of your own choice.

5. If you prefer, study one or more of the following chapters before you write your song.

6. Use extra paper for extra lyrics, or write at the bottom of the page if space permits.

TITLE

COMPOSER(S)

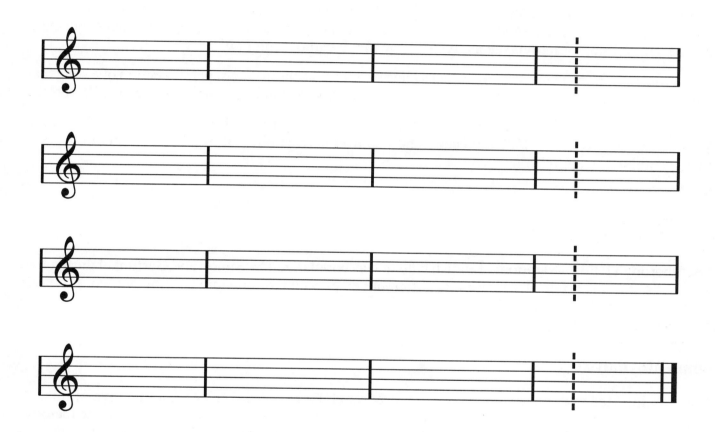

THE AAA "VERSE-CHORUS" SONG FORM

Some AAA songs use the same melody for the verse *and* chorus. It is best to consider such songs to be a variation on AAA, not a "true" verse-chorus form. This is because a true chorus has a different melody than the verse. Examples of *AAA "verse-chorus"* songs include: "Born in the U.S.A." (Bruce Springsteen), "Wild Side of Life," "Old Time Rock and Roll," "Words of Love," and "Waltz Across Texas."

THE AAA WITH A REFRAIN SONG FORM

Form AAA with a refrain is very similar to form AAA. The difference is the addition of the refrain—one or more lines sung at the end of each verse. Usually, the lyrics in each refrain are the same, but there can be some slight variation (see analysis following "Scarborough Fair").

Sometimes a refrain is inaccurately called a chorus, but a true chorus is a separate section of a song that contrasts with the verse. Conversely, the refrain is actually a conclusion or resolution of the verse.

Examples of AAA tunes with a refrain are "Memphis Blues Again," "Here Comes the Sun," "Funny How Time Slips Away," "I Fall to Pieces," and "California Dreamin'." It is quite common for the title to be contained in the refrain.

SCARBOROUGH FAIR

"Scarborough Fair," a traditional English ballad, was popularized by Simon and Garfunkel during the 1960s "folk-rock" boom. There are four different verses on the Simon and Garfunkel record; I have provided lyrics for two verses here.

Comment/Analysis

The refrain at the end of the first verse of "Scarborough Fair" is "*she once was* a true love of mine." The refrain at the end of the second verse is "*then she'll be* a true love of mine." However, the melody is the same for each lyric. Note also that the title is *not* included in the refrain here, a situation that is more the exception than the norm.

Recommended Listening

"Scarborough Fair," *Simon & Garfunkel's Greatest Hits*, Columbia KC 31350.

Scarborough Fair

Example of Form AAA with Refrain

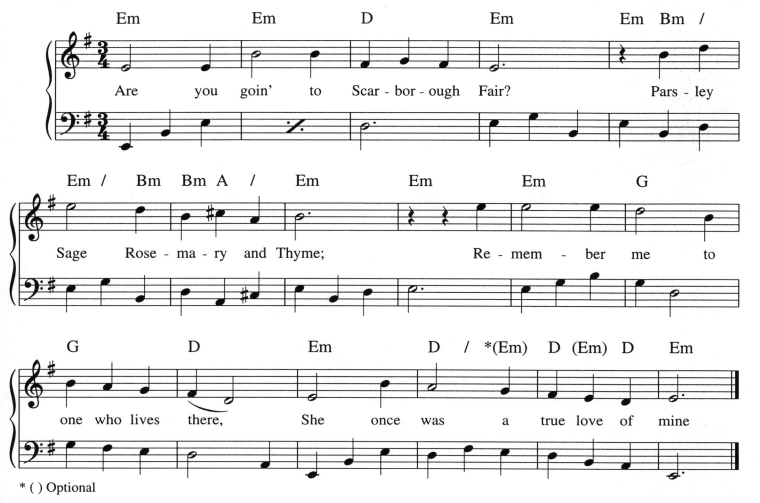

Are you goin' to Scar - bor - ough Fair? Pars - ley

Sage Rose - ma - ry and Thyme; Re - mem - ber me to

one who lives there, She once was a true love of mine

* ( ) Optional

Additional Verse:

Tell her to make me a cambric shirt,
Parsley Sage, Rosemary and Thyme;
Without any seam or fine needlework,
Then she'll be a true love of mine.

GUITAR CHORDS

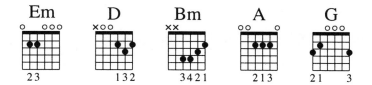

ARRANGING SESSION: AAA WITH REFRAIN

This sketch is a typical example of an AAA with refrain song arranged for performance or recording.

Instrumental Intro.	Verse 1	Verse 2
4 Bars	**16 Bars**	**16 Bars**

Instrumental Solo	Verse 3	Coda
16 Bars	**16 Bars**	**8 Bars**

Comment/Analysis

1. The refrain, located at the end of each verse, often occupies four full measures.
2. The title is often contained in the refrain.
3. The solo may be played over the same chord progression used in the verse.
4. Songs arranged for vocal groups and "feature" vocalists often place minimal emphasis on instrumental solos.
5. The coda often contains several repetitions of the title.

SONGWRITING PRACTICE
FORM: AAA WITH REFRAIN
LENGTH: 16 BARS

Write three verses of lyrics with a refrain at the end of each verse. Choose your own key and time signature.

Tips

1. Be sure you understand exactly what the refrain is before you write your lyrics (study the tunes listed on p. 16).
2. Try to make your storyline evolve as the verses unfold.
3. The refrain could occupy the last four bars of each verse, but this is up to you.
4. Sometimes a "surprise" ending is effective in the final verse, but this is not essential.
5. If you prefer, study one or more of the following chapters before you write your song.

TITLE

COMPOSER(S)

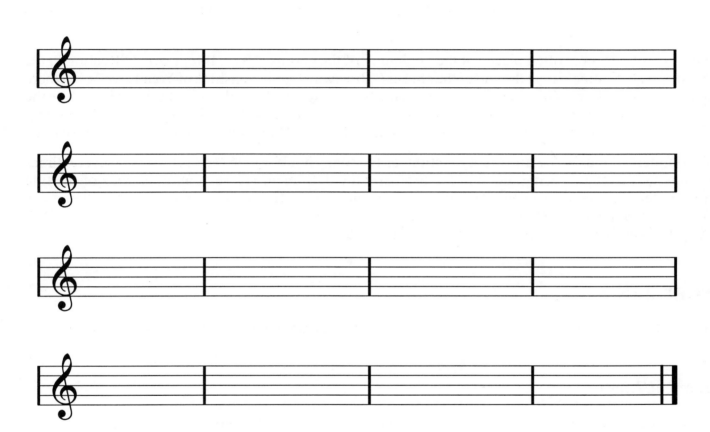

THE <u>VERSE-CHORUS</u> SONG FORM

The *verse-chorus* song form, sometimes called AB, is today's most popular compositional format. Like the verses in the AAA form, the verses here are used to develop the storyline. The chorus provides lyrical and musical contrast, restates the song's meaning from a different perspective, and often repeats the title or "hook." The verse leads logically to the chorus, and frequently the music is arranged so that a dynamic "punch" occurs at the beginning of the chorus. While the lyrics in the verse change each time, the chorus lyrics usually remain the same. The verse-chorus format is used in instrumental music ("St. Thomas" by Sonny Rollins) and, more often, for popular vocal music.

The most common arrangement of a verse-chorus tune has one or more verses preceding the first chorus ("Whiter Shade of Pale," "Almost Persuaded," and "Wild Thing"). However, any variation is possible; for example, the songs "Another Saturday Night" and "Hello Mary Lou" *begin* with the chorus. Another variation is found in the Beatles' recording of "Can't Buy Me Love," which starts with *part of the chorus.*

The V/C title is most often placed at the beginning of the chorus ("Bye, Bye, Love," "Reeling in the Years," and "Nadine") or at the end of the chorus ("Runaway," and "Sunshine of Your Love"), but there are variations. Some V/C titles appear at both the beginning and the end of the chorus ("That'll Be the Day," "Layla," "Peggy Sue," and "I Will Always Love You"). The title of "Rocky Top" and "I Fought the Law" are in both the verse and chorus, and the title of "A Hard Day's Night" is in the verse only.

In commercial music, the title often functions as the song "hook" (p. 46) and is repeated several times ("Suzy Q") so that it is ingrained in the listener's mind. Sometimes, several repetitions of the title appear near the end of the song ("California Dreamin'," and "Hey Jude"), and sometimes the title is mercilessly repeated to the point of annoyance ("Peggy Sue" is sung more than 25 times). In "I Will Always Love You," the title, sung twice, *is* the chorus.

ANGEL BAND

The traditional gospel song "Angel Band" is used to illustrate the verse-chorus song format.

Comment/Analysis

"Angel Band" contains the following elements of the "classic" AB (verse-chorus) song form.

1. The song starts with the verse.
2. The title is contained in the first line of the chorus.
3. The melody in the chorus is different than the melody in the verse.
4. The harmonic progression (chords) in the chorus is different than the harmony in the verse.
5. The words change from verse to verse.
6. The verse is used to develop the story or theme.
7. The words in each chorus are the same.
8. The 16-bar section (verse or chorus) is a standard length in both traditional and popular music.

Recommended Listening

A short instrumental version of "Angel Band" is on the *Civil War Original Soundtrack Recording*, Elektra 979256-2.

Angel Band

Example of Verse-Chorus Song Form

come and a - round me stand;

Take me a - way on your snow - y wings, to

my im - mor - tal home.

Additional Verse:

Oh bear my longing heart to Him,
Who bled and died for me;
Whose blood now cleanses from all sins,
And gives me victory.

Guitar Chords

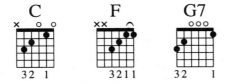

ARRANGING SESSION: VERSE-CHORUS

This sketch is a typical example of a verse-chorus tune arranged for performance or recording.

Intro.	Verse 1	Chorus	Verse 2	Chorus
4 Bars	**16 Bars**	**8 Bars**	**16 Bars**	**8 Bars**

(Instrumental)

Instrumental Solo	Verse 3	Chorus	Coda
8 Bars	**16 Bars**	**8 Bars**	**: 16 Bars :**

(Repeat and Fade)

Comment/Analysis

1. A simple instrumental <u>vamp</u> (chording or picking pattern on the tonic chord) is often sufficient for a short intro, particularly for a strong singer.

2. It is quite common to sing two verses before singing the first chorus.

3. The chords for the instrumental could be from the verse or chorus, depending on which one seems to be the most suitable.

4. Sometimes, backup vocal groups hum the melody of the verse or chorus as an alternative to an instrumental solo.

5. An effective way to arrange a "fade-out" ending (coda) is to have the singer repeat the last line of the chorus over and over. This is especially effective if the last line of the chorus includes the song title.

SONGWRITING PRACTICE
FORM: VERSE-CHORUS
LENGTH: 8 TO 16 BARS IN EACH SECTION

1. Write a verse-chorus song with melody and/or lyrics.

2. Use either eight or sixteen bars for each section. It is okay to have a sixteen-bar verse and an eight-bar chorus (or vice-versa). Fill in the barlines as needed.

3. Try to place your title at the beginning of the chorus. If you wish, place it at the end of the chorus also.

4. Write three verses, each with its own set of lyrics, but use the same lyrics for each chorus. Use a separate sheet of paper for your second and third verses.

5. Be sure to make the chorus *contrast* with the verse by using a different melody, harmonic progression, rhythm, key, viewpoint, etc.

6. Choose your own key and time signature.

7. If you prefer, study one or more of the following chapters before you write your song.

8. If you have been studying the "arranger's session" sketches, try preparing a similar model for your own song.

TITLE

COMPOSER(S)

THE BLUES

Perhaps no other form of American music has been as influential as the *blues*. Originating in the rural South, the blues form has gone on to influence folk, pop, country, and jazz styles all over the world.

The essence of the blues is a 12-bar verse that is harmonized with the I7, IV7, and V7 chords (C7, F7, and G7 in the key of C). Contained within the twelve-measure *blues progression* are three four-bar phrases (see "Backporch Blues"). Lyrically, the first phrase is stated (mes. 1-4), repeated (mes. 5-8), and then followed by a different phrase–often ironic in tone–which is used to conclude the verse (mes. 9-12). This lyric structure is called AAB. Blues melodies contain flatted thirds, flatted sevenths, and—sometimes—flatted fifths. These notes are often "bent" or "shaded" by the vocalist (or instrumentalist) to approach or approximate the natural pitch of the interval.

Rhythmically, blues tunes tend to be set to a shuffle beat ♪♪ = ♪³♪, a 12/8 triplet beat, or a combination of the two ("Blues with a Feeling"). However, many blues are played in "straight" time as well ("Killing Floor," and "Born in Chicago"). Although most blues are in 12/8—or 4/4—some jazz blues are in 3/4 ("All Blues" by Miles Davis; "West Coast Blues" by Wes Montgomery). All of these rhythms are explained in Chapter Seven.

Not only the backbone of jazz, the blues form has also been borrowed by all of the popular musical styles. Examples include "Steam Roller Blues" (James Taylor), "Red House" (Jimi Hendrix), "Working Man Blues" (Merle Haggard), "Johnny B. Goode" (Chuck Berry), and "Hound Dog" (popularized by Big Mama Thornton and Elvis). The early rock and roll stars such as Elvis Presley, Bill Haley, Chuck Berry, Carl Perkins, and Jerry Lee Lewis were all heavily influenced by the blues.

Many blues songs are written in minor keys ("The Thrill is Gone"), and there are many other variations such as 8-bar blues ("Key to the Highway"), 16-bar blues ("Watermelon Man"), and 24-bar blues ("Big Boss Man"). Some blues tunes have a "chorus" that is sung to the same melody as the verse ("Hound Dog"); other blues progressions have distinct melodies for both the verse and the chorus ("The Stroll").

Certain tunes contain the word <u>blues</u> in the title, but they are not true blues in a structural sense ("The Birth of the Blues," and "Limehouse Blues").

Blues songs often contain melancholic—or even tragic—lyrics, often in regard to love affairs and relationships ("I Got a Mind to Give Up Living"). However, blues lyrics actually cover a wide range of everyday concerns and attitudes, including humor ("Nobody's Business"), wanderlust ("Ramblin' on My Mind"), justice ("Boxcar Shorty"), religion ("Keep Your Lamp Trimmed and Burning") and hokum ("Salty Dog Blues").

BACKPORCH BLUES

The next musical example, "Backporch Blues," illustrates many of the common characteristics of the 12-bar blues.

Comment/Analysis

1. Note that the first lyrical phrase in measures 1-4 is repeated in measures 5-8, and the verse ends with a different, concluding phrase in measures 9-12.

2. The flatted third of the C scale (E♭) is used is measures 1, 2, 5, 6, and 10.

3. The flatted seventh (B♭) is used in measure 9.

4. The flatted fifth (G♭) is used in measure 10.

5. Flatted thirds, fifths, and sevenths are known as "blue notes."

6. Be sure to interpret each pair of eighth notes as the first and third units of an eighth-note triplet figure. To correctly interpret and feel the rhythm, divide each beat into three equal parts (see Chapter Seven).

7. More advanced players will wish to experiment with other chord voicings in order to obtain the smoothest transitions.

Recommended Listening

Muddy Waters, *The Chess Box*, Chess 80002.
Howlin' Wolf, *His Greatest Sides*, Volume One, Chess 9107.

Backporch Blues

Example of 12-Bar Blues

L. McCabe

BASIC RHYTHM FOR BACKPORCH BLUES:

GUITAR CHORDS

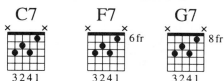

ARRANGING SESSION: 12-BAR BLUES

Basic Arranging Principles

1. The most typical introduction for the blues is to start with an instrumental solo to the chords in measures 9 - 12.

2. Almost as often, the entire 12-bar progression is used for an instrumental introduction.

3. For a rock effect, play the blues in straight time with evenly accented eighth notes, and add distortion to the guitar.

4. Standard endings can be easily learned by copying from blues records.

SONGWRITING PRACTICE
FORM: BLUES
LENGTH: 12 BARS

1. Write a 12-bar blues with at least three verses of lyrics. If the blues is entirely new to you, feel free to use the melody of "Backporch Blues."

2. Use the C blues scale for your melody (C-E♭-F-G♭-G-B♭-C).

3. Be sure to do some serious listening to blues recordings before writing your lyrics.

4. For now, adhere to the standard AAB lyric format. As you gain more experience, you can experiment with variations.

5. If you prefer, study one or more of the following chapters before you write your own song.

TITLE

COMPOSER(S)

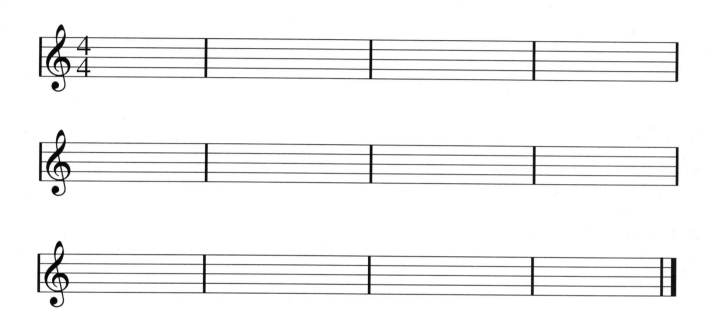

THE <u>AABA</u> SONG FORM

The *AABA song* has been with us for many years, and it continues to endure as a vehicle for compositions in all popular styles. The "classic" or standard AABA model looks like this:

8 BARS	8 BARS	8 BARS	8 BARS
A1	A2	B	A3
	Repeat of A1 Leads to B	Contrasting section Leads back to A	Reiteration of A1 (or A2)

The main melody (or theme) occurs in the A sections, and the B section is used for variety or contrast. Typically, the "hook" is placed in one or more of the A sections. The melody is basically the same in each A section, although it may vary at the end of A2 in order to connect smoothly to B.

The B section—also called the *bridge* or the *middle eight*—differs from a chorus in that it is a <u>component</u> of the overall AABA form (a chorus is an independent section). The bridge (B) contains a melody that is different from the A part, and it may also be different rhythmically and/or harmonically. Some B sections move into a new key altogether. The B lyrics elaborate on the storyline, often from a different perspective.

Several standard methods are used to create a different perspective in the B section; for instance, the time frame might be changed (past to future, present to past, etc.). Also, the pronouns could change focus, say from the first person (I or we) to the second person (you) or third person (he, she, or they.) Changing the mood of the lyrics is another common technique; this can be achieved by changing from calm (A sections) to excited (B section), happy to remorseful, and so on. Changing perspective helps to hold and increase the interest of the listener.

It is not necessary to adhere strictly to the 32-bar (8-8-8-8) form; for example, "Yesterday" by The Beatles is an AABA tune with only seven bars in each A section (7-7-8-7).

Ever since the mass-production of recorded music began in the 1920s, the AABA has been one of the most enduring song forms, as evidenced by the following examples:

1920s   "Ain't Misbehavin'"
1930s   "As Time Goes By"
1940s   "Autumn Leaves"
1950s   "True Love Ways"
1960s   "Yesterday"
1970s   "Here You Come Again"
1980s   "I Won't Stand in Your Way"

The above list is only a small sample of the great number of AABA tunes popularized over the last several decades. Many composers have made extensive use of the AABA; for example, "Satin Doll," "Solitude," and "Take the A Train" are only a few of many AABA songs composed by the great Duke Ellington.

DOWN AT LES' PLACE

"Down at Les' Place" is an original composition that will help you understand the AABA song form. Be sure to listen to some other AABA tunes so that you will have a firm grasp of this very important form.

Comment/Analysis

1. The melody is the same in each A section. The G7 chord at the end of the second A section leads A2 into the bridge (B).

2. Note that the B section has a different melody and chord progression than the A sections.

3. "Down at Les' Place" contains 8 bars per section.

Down At Les' Place

L. McCabe

Example of AABA Song Form

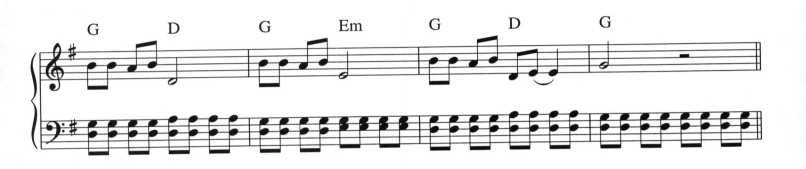

GUITAR CHORDS

33

ARRANGING SESSION: AABA

This sketch is a typical example of an AABA song, arranged for performance or recording.

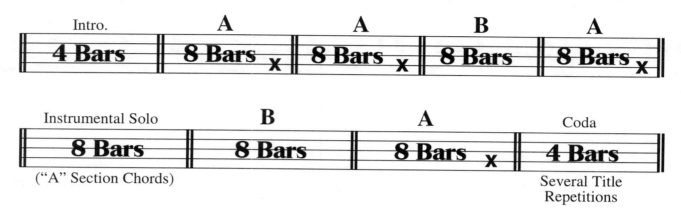

Comment/Analysis

1. The title, indicated by the x, typically appears at the end of one or more of the A sections.
2. The title is also repeated several times in the coda.
3. The instrumental solo here is played over the A section chords. The solo begins after the first complete AABA section.
4. Note how the AABA sequence is broken up after the solo. This format creates variety and helps to keep the recording time limited to four minutes or less.
5. The instrumental is not always played to chords from the A (or B) section. Sometimes an instrumental *interlude* is played to a different chord progression altogether.
6. The instrumental section may fulfill any of the following objectives:
   a. To showcase the playing skills of one (or more) of the musicians.
   b. To provide a change of pace.
   c. To modulate to a new key.
   d. To provide a smooth connection to the next section.

SONGWRITING PRACTICE
FORM: AABA
LENGTH: 32 BARS

1. Write an AABA tune (melody and/or lyrics) with eight bars in each section.
2. Use the key and time signature of your choice.
3. Make sure that the B section is different from the A sections (use any combination of the techniques you have studied here).
4. Place your title in the last line of one (or more) of the A sections. Omit your title from the bridge (B) so that it offers a different perspective.
5. Be sure to study sheet music and recordings of AABA tunes from 1920 to the present.
6. If you wish, come back and write your song after you have studied the next several chapters.

THE <u>ABAC</u> SONG FORM

Like the AABA song, the main part of the *ABAC song* is the A sections. The standard ABAC length is eight bars per section—32 bars in all—but this can vary. Usually, the title is placed at the beginning of the A section, or at the end of B or C. C may bear some resemblance to B, but on close inspection it is shown to have its own identity. Often, the hook is located in the C section, following a build-up.

Examples of ABAC tunes are: "Fools Rush In," "Limehouse Blues," "Days of Wine and Roses," "When Your Lover Has Gone," "Laura," and "This Love of Mine." Other song forms with three distinct sections are discussed in the miscellaneous category at the end of this chapter.

ARRANGING SESSION: ABAC

This sketch is a typical example of an ABAC song, arranged for performance or recording.

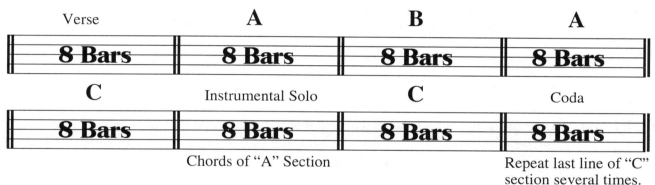

Comment/Analysis

1. Many ABAC tunes were originally show tunes ("Stardust," "Blue Moon") with a separate verse at the beginning of the song. (This technique was used for AABA songs as well.) This allowed the stage performer to get the audience in the mood of the tune—sometimes in a melodramatic fashion—before the band "kicked in." Nowadays, these verses have gone out of style and are often dropped from the performance.

2. Jazz players refer to the cumulative length of ABAC (and AABA, etc.) tunes as the "chorus."

3. ABAC tunes are less common than AABA compositions, but you will find plenty of them if you do some exploring. Tip: Ricky Nelson, Frank Sinatra, Glenn Miller, Mildred Bailey, Lionel Hampton, and many others have recorded the ABAC classic "Fools Rush In."

Recommended Listening

"When Your Lover Has Gone," *Linda Ronstadt with Nelson Riddle, Lush Life*, Asylum 60387-1.

SONGWRITING PRACTICE

Those who wish to may write the melody and/or lyrics to an ABAC song. Use eight-bar sections, and be sure to analyze several recorded examples to gain insight into this form.

MISCELLANEOUS SONG FORMS

ABCD

Comparatively rare, the *ABCD song,* also called *through-composed,* has four musical sections. In this style, the B, C, and D sections tend to be variations or developments of the initial A section. ABCD song examples include "You'll Never Walk Alone," "I'll See You Again," "Autumn in New York," "April in Paris," and "You Do Something to Me." Elvis Presley's recording of "You'll Never Walk Alone" on the Double Dynamite LP (Pickwick DL2-5001) is a good place to begin your study of this form.

AABA WITH BRIDGE

Any song form is subject to modification, and recently the longer airplay limits (four minutes) have allowed songwriters to add new sections to traditional song forms. A case in point is "Every Breath You Take" by The Police; in this song, a C section is used as a bridge after the initial AABA to yield the result A/A/B/A/C/B/A/A (coda). This song form could be called an *AABA with bridge.*

VERSE-CHORUS WITH BRIDGE

A bridge may also be used in the verse-chorus format to provide three distinct musical sections; this form is called a *verse-chorus with bridge.* A good example of this style is "Right Time of the Night" by Jennifer Warnes. This song may be sketched as follows:

VS/CH/VS/CH/BRIDGE/CH/CH (CODA)

"Sgt. Pepper's Lonely Hearts Club Band" by The Beatles looks like this:

VS/CH/BRIDGE/VS/CODA

SUGGESTED PROJECTS

1. Compare any standard sheet of music to a recording of the same song, and attempt to answer these questions:
   A) Does the sheet music include all of the sections of the recorded arrangement?
   B) Is the sheet music arranged in the same sequence as the recording?
   C) If the answer to either A or B is "no," what is missing from the sheet music (why is it incomplete)?
   D) Is the sheet music scored in the same key as the recording?
2. Create an "arranger's sketch" from any recording.
3. Identify at least one recorded example of each of the following song forms:
   A)   AAA
   B)   AAA with refrain
   C)   Verse/Chorus
   D)   The Blues
   E)   AABA

3

SONG TITLES, THEMES, AND LYRICS

All good songs start with a good idea, and good ideas can be found almost anywhere. The next step is to develop a good idea into a great song. To accomplish this, songwriters use certain literary and poetic devices such as rhymes, figurative language, and point of view to create interesting lyrics and a memorable storyline.

This chapter provides an overview of the techniques the professionals use to write the songs that you and I call our "favorites." After you master these techniques, perhaps some of your songs will become "favorites," too.

IDEAS AND INSPIRATION

Inspiration comes from within, but an idea can come from anywhere. The artistic mind has the ability to recognize the possibilities of an idea, and the skill to develop it to its fullest potential. The following list shows many ways to generate ideas for song titles, themes, and lyrics.

1. First-hand experiences such as hobbies, conversations, work and leisure activities.
2. Printed materials: books, newspapers, magazines, sheet music, etc.
3. Broadcast and audio/visual industry: radio, television, films.
4. Street signs.
5. Old sayings (adages, proverbs, etc.).
6. Seasonal, patriotic, and religious events and experiences.
7. Spontaneous ideas that seem to come "out of nowhere" (keep a microcassette recorder handy for these fortunate moments!).
8. Names of people and places.
9. Recordings of all types.
10. Research at the public library.
11. Real-life events of other people both current and historical.
12. Conscientious application of the principles of music to an original work.

SONG TITLES

A song title can be about almost anything, but it should reveal something about the song itself. In addition, the title should be as original as possible. It also helps if the title is easy to remember.

The following list of 75 songs shows many everyday sources that may be used to generate ideas for titles.

Source	Title
1. A sign	"Detour"
2. A question	"Do You Love Me?"
3. Hope	"All I Need is a Miracle"
4. An opinion	"You're No Good"
5. Slang expression	"Yakety-Yak"
6. Living quarters	"White Room"
7. A day	"Monday, Monday"
8. A color	"Whiter Shade of Pale"
9. A name	"Sunny"
10. Love	"I Honestly Love You"
11. A command	"Do It Again"
12. A modified expression	"Total Eclipse of the Heart"
13. A holiday	"Happy Birthday"

14.	An emotion	"I'm in the Mood for Love"
15.	Eternity	"The Twelfth of Never"
16.	Travel	"Ticket to Ride"
17.	A prediction	"I'll Fall in Love Tonight"
18.	Faith	"Amazing Grace"
19.	A relative	"Cousin of Mine"
20.	A predicament	"Stuck In the Middle With You"
21.	Sports or hobby	"Surfin' U.S.A."
22.	Gratitude	"You've Made Me So Very Happy"
23.	A season	"Summertime"
24.	Dreaming	"These Dreams"
25.	A character	"Bad, Bad, Leroy Brown"
26.	A state	"Sweet Home Alabama"
27.	A nickname	"Sweet Little Sixteen"
28.	A dance	"The Twist"
29.	A promise	"Forever I Do"
30.	Self-characterization	"I'm a Lover"
31.	Change	"The Times They Are Changin'"
32.	Compliment	"Three Times a Lady"
33.	Contentment	"Top of the World"
34.	An occupation	"Paperback Writer"
35.	Nature	"Ebb Tide"
36.	Time of day	"Midnight Hour"
37.	Memories	"My Old School"
38.	Correspondence	"The Letter"
39.	Melancholia	"Misty"
40.	A warning	"Watch My .44"
41.	Wealth	"Rich Girl"
42.	The past	"Yesterday"
43.	The future	"In the Year 2525"
44.	Extraterrestrial	"Mr. Spaceman"
45.	A declaration	"Tonight, I Celebrate My Love"
46.	Rebellion	"Born to be Wild"
47.	One-word titles	"Still"; "Cherish"; "Traces"
48.	Family relations	"Mama Tried"
49.	Cheating	"Runaround Sue"
50.	Nostalgia	"Old Time Rock and Roll"
51.	Children	"Mary Wore Her Red Dress"
52.	Introspection	"Look to Your Soul"

53. Attire	"Blue Suede Shoes"
54. War	"The Cruel War"
55. Cars	"Mustang Sally"
56. A month	"April Showers"
57. Drinking	"The Bottle Let Me Down"
58. Humor	"Bony Moronie"
59. Sidekicks	"Me and Bobby McGee"
60. Tragedy	"The Carrol County Accident"
61. Musicians	"Minstrel of the Dawn"
62. Surprise	"Without a Word of Warning"
63. Impatience	"Tired of Waiting for You"
64. An image	"Crystal Blue Persuasions"
65. Restlessness	"I Gotta Keep On Movin'"
66. Blues	"Roadhouse Blues"
67. Matrimony	"To the Aisle"
68. Reunions	"Daddy's Home"
69. Politics	"Superbird"
70. A resolution	"I'll Never Fall in Love Again"
71. Loneliness	"All Alone Am I"
72. Ethnic title/theme	"Soul Man"
73. Hardship	"Busted"
74. Jewelry	"This Diamond Ring"
75. A flavor	"Tutti-Frutti"

Needless to say, many of the song titles can be credited to more than one original source. The main idea here is to help you see that ideas can come from almost anywhere and anything; it is your task as a songwriter to recognize, exploit, and develop good ideas.

THE THEME

The unfolding of the story line is known as the *plot* or *theme*. Because a song's title usually tells something about the story line, many subjects for themes may be found in song titles. Any broad topic can be reduced to more specific categories from which a specific theme may be developed. For instance, love may be viewed as a broad category from which a number of more specific topics such as happiness, marriage, sadness, separation, uncertainty, reconciliation, etc. may be selected.

CENTRAL THEME/SUB THEMES

Your song should have a *central theme* that comes into focus early. Try to keep the action moving while you develop the central theme. You must tell a complete story, so avoid overly complicated themes that cannot be resolved in a reasonable amount of time.

Choosing a specific theme does not mean that your song cannot branch out a little. Professional writers are skilled at connecting *sub-themes* to the central theme. For example, "Bad, Bad, Leroy Brown" (Jim Croce) is mainly about a bully on Chicago's Southside, but the song also contains sub-themes dealing with vice, male/female relationships, jealousy, and poetic justice.

TIME-FRAME

If there is a passage of time, be sure the lyrics distinctly show how the story moves from one *time-frame* to another. The plot must be developed within the proper time-frame, which can range from just a few minutes to many years. "Silhouettes" tells of events that occur within a couple of hours, while "April, Come She Will" takes place over a period of several months. Bobby Goldsboro's "Autumn of My Life" shows how a clever writer can successfully condense the passage of many years into one short song.

LOGICAL SEQUENCE

Arrange the events in a logical sequence. If someone is driving a car in one phrase and walking in the next, be sure to tell how they got outside of the car.

CONFLICT/RESOLUTION

The story line should contain *conflicts that demand resolution*. When properly set up, conflicts are an effective way to grab and hold listeners' attention. Resolutions give the listener a sense of relief and personal involvement.

SURPRISE ENDING

The element of surprise is just as effective in songs as it is in novels and movies. Try writing a tune with a *surprise* ending ("Silhouettes," "Memphis").

COMMERCIAL CONSIDERATIONS

If you are writing for the popular market, you must keep certain *commercial considerations* in mind. Recordings that exceed four minutes in length are often unacceptable for commercial airplay, so try to make every word count. Also, be sensitive to trends, and keep your themes and lyrics up-to-date.

THOUGHTS ON WRITING LYRICS

1. Know who your intended listener is, and write for the listener. Connect with your listener, entertain your listener, and communicate with your listener.

2. Use language and ideas that your listener can understand. The listener is not interested in technical data or personal opinions that he or she cannot relate to. Try to touch universal emotions.

3. The lyrics should be completely believable—unless they are intentionally ridiculous or exaggerated ("Alley Oop," "The Purple People Eater").

4. Get to the point as soon as possible. Don't put your listener on a slow boat to China.

5. Be sure that the lyrics consistently tie in to a central theme or idea (of course, there can be sub-themes as well).

6. It is a good idea to collect phrases and develop them as related ideas emerge.

7. Accenting is important. Usually, the first downbeat of the measure is accented. Often, the third downbeat is also accented (in 4/4 time). In addition, some lyrics will be syncopated (accented on the upbeat).

8. The lyrics should flow naturally without seeming forced. Be sure that the lyrics make logical musical phrases. Non-musician lyricists should acquire a feel for phrasing by singing along with records and learning about the basic song forms. Each lyrical phrase, like a complete sentence, should have meaning within itself.

9. Use words that are easy to understand, but be descriptive and avoid trite, overused, or too-plain expressions. For example, "My Mighty GTO" is more colorful and descriptive than "my car."

10. Strive for originality in expression, but keep it musical. A song is a musical composition, not a poem.

FIGURATIVE LANGUAGE

Figurative language refers to the use of words in a manner that is inconsistent with their normal, literal use or application. There are several categories of figurative language—each known as a *figure of speech*—that allow one to describe something in a novel, imaginative way, and more vividly than the use of ordinary terms would allow. The most common figures of speech—*similes* and *metaphors*—are described here along with several others.

1. A *simile* states an explicit comparison between two dissimilar things by using the words *like* or *as* ("Your Love is Like a Heatwave").

2. A *metaphor* is an implied comparison which equates one thing with another *without using the words like* or *as* ("You Are My Sunshine"). *Are* and *is* are the words most often used to set up metaphors.

3. *Personification* is the attribution of human qualities to nonhuman things ("Moody River").

4. An *overstatement*—also known as *hyperbole*—is a deliberate, obvious exaggeration intended to make or support a particular point of view ("Eight Days a Week," "I Fall to Pieces").

5. *Understatement* is used to express a thought or emotion in very restrained terms ("It's Not Over 'Til It's Over").

6. *Apostrophe* means to address a deceased or absent person, place or thing ("Roll Over, Beethoven," "Bye, Bye, Love").

7. *Irony* is an expression or suggestion meant to be understood in the opposite sense of its literal meaning ("It Never Rains in Southern California").

8. An *oxymoron* is the combining of contradictory words for a paradoxical effect ("The Roaring Silence").

9. A *pun* is a word or saying that is modified to create a new, often humorous meaning ("U.S. Male").

RHYMES AND RHYMING

PERFECT RHYMES

The Random House dictionary defines a *rhyme* as "a word agreeing with another in terminal sound." A *perfect rhyme* consists of two (or more) words that have the same terminal sound, preceded by consonantal sounds (consonants) that are different. Thus, *win* and *tin, win* and *gin,* and *win* and *bin* are all perfect rhymes.

IDENTITIES

Words having the same terminal sound, preceded by the <u>same</u> consonant, are known as *identities*:

amplify/simplify   corn/scorn   reply/multiply

Identities are considered to be weak, and should be avoided wherever possible. Two pairs of identities are found in the first verse of Robert Burns' "Flow Gently Sweet Afton":

> Flow Gently, Sweet Afton, among thy green *braes,*
> Flow gently, I'll sing thee a song in thy *praise;*
> My Mary's a-sleep by the murmuring *stream,*
> Flow gently, Sweet Afton, disturb not her *dream.*

CONSONANCE

Consonance—also known as *off rhyme*—is the name for identical consonant sounds which follow different vowels:

men/done   past/nest

Here is an example of consonance, taken from the folk-blues tune "Things About Goin' My Way":

> The pot was empty,
> The cupboard *bare*;
> I said, Mama, Mama,
> What's goin' on *here*?

Consonance is a common technique in both contemporary music and poetry.

ASSONANCE—also known as *near-rhyme, lazy rhyme*, and *vowel rhyme*—involves a repetition of the same vowel sound ("<u>A</u>chy Br<u>ea</u>ky Heart"). The following example is from "The Gallows Pole":

> Papa, did you bring me silver?
> Papa, did you bring me g<u>o</u>ld?
> Did you come to see the hangin',
> By The Gallows P<u>o</u>le?

Not uncommon in popular music, assonance is used in the lyrics of "It's Still Rock and Roll to Me," "Blackbird," and many other tunes.

Table 1 (below) summarizes perfect rhymes, identities, consonance, and assonance.

COLLOQUIAL RHYMES

Colloquial rhymes contain words that are mispronounced by dropping letters, ignoring sounds, etc.

   ruin/doin' (doing);   kept/'cept (except);   faster/massa (master)

Colloquial rhymes and near-rhymes are best used in tunes that have an informal or humorous tone.

TWO-WORD RHYMES

Rhymes sometimes involve the use of two words:

   My son/Tyson;   May Day/payday

Table 1: Perfect rhymes, identities, consonance, and assonance

Rhymes	Identities	Consonance	Assonance (vowel rhymes)
Time/Dime	Time/Thyme	Time/Dame	Time/Fine
Aflame/Tame	Aflame/Inflame	Aflame/Dime	Aflame/Main
Sight/Flight	Sight/Cite	Sight/Late	Sight/Hide
Lied/Died	Lied/Plied	Lied/Fade	Lied/I'm

BASIC RHYME SCHEMES

END RHYME

End rhyme occurs at the end of the lines, as in the following example from "Greensleeves":

Line 1   Alas, my love, you do me wrong,

    2   To cast me off discourteously;

    3   And I have loved you so long,

    4   Delighting in your company.

The end rhymes in the above example are found in lines 1 & 3 and 2 & 4. End rhymes can also occur on lines 1 & 2 and 3 & 4 (see the verse from "Flow Gently, Sweet Afton" on page 43).

Another common end-rhyme variation in the four-line stanza or verse: Lines 1 & 3 do not rhyme, but lines 2 & 4 do ("City of New Orleans").

Sometimes, repetition is used in this scheme, as in lines 1 & 3 of the "Tom Dooley" chorus:

Line 1   Hang down your head Tom Dooley,

    2   Hang down your head and cry;

    3   Hang down your head Tom Dooley,

    4   Poor boy, you're bound to die.

INNER RHYME

Also known as *internal rhyme,* an *inner rhyme* is contained within the phrase, as shown here:

> At *noon* the sun,
>
> Is in the sky;
>
> The *moon* is there,
>
> At evening time.

TIPS FOR EFFECTIVE RHYMING

1. It is often effective to use different rhyme schemes for different song sections. For instance, if you are writing a verse-chorus tune, try end rhymes for the verses, and inner rhymes for the chorus (or vice-versa).

2. Try to make sure the second rhyme-word has more emotional "punch" than the first one.

   date/hate   for/war   bet/threat

3. A rhyming dictionary is quite helpful. You should be able to locate one at your local bookstore or public library.

POINT OF VIEW

Point of view refers to the source of the story. The viewpoint can be told from the perspective of the *first person* (I or we), the *second person* (you), or the *third person* (he or she).

THE FIRST PERSON

The *first person* can have a known identity ("Duke of Earl") or an anonymous identity ("Swingin' Doors"); either way, the story line is basically centered on the "I" perspective. Another first person viewpoint is the "we" viewpoint, which means "you and I" ("Together Again"). Finally, the "collective we" viewpoint refers to "all of us" ("We Shall Not Be Moved"). First-person lyrics allow the listener to become the "I" (or one of the "we's"); this helps him or her to identify with the message. First-person accounts should reflect universal emotions and concerns that many people can relate to.

THE SECOND PERSON

The *second person* viewpoint places the focus on a particular you; "you" could be a person ("Big Boss Man"), place ("Missouri"), or thing ("Moody River"). Here, "you" is the person, place or thing to whom the lyrics are sung, and the singer takes the role of an acquaintance—often unnamed—who is providing feedback by singing to, or thinking about, the second person. The Eagles song, "Desperado," is a good example of a second-person viewpoint.

THE THIRD PERSON

The singer with a *third person* point of view (he/she) is an observer or narrator telling a story about another person or place. Such songs often deal with universal emotions—love, loneliness, etc.— through the experiences of the main subject. Well-written lyrics allow the listener to relate to the character (and, hopefully, head for the record store to buy the song). "The Pilgrim: Chapter 33" by Kris Kristofferson is a great third-person tune, as is "Eleanor Rigby" by The Beatles.

THE HOOK

The *hook* is a device used extensively in commercial songwriting. Designed to "catch" the attention of the listener, a hook may be either lyrical or instrumental. A *lyrical hook* (also called a storyline look) is a word or phrase that is used repetitiously throughout the song; many lyrical hooks are also the title ("Let it Be").

Often used as an introduction, an *instrumental hook* is a unique riff or phrase that comes to be associated with a particular song ("Dragnet"). Like the lyrical hook, the instrumental hook is likely to be repeated several times throughout the song.

A good hook—lyrical or instrumental—should not only be "catchy," but it should also be easy to remember. This goal is helped, of course, by a generous amount of—some say an overdose of— repetition.

MISCELLANEOUS TECHNIQUES FOR TITLES AND LYRICS

NONSTANDARD LANGUAGE

Colloquial speech and *slang* are in a category known as *nonstandard language*. Although it is difficult to pinpoint the precise differences between the two, colloquial speech is generally regarded as that which is used in everyday, informal conversation and writing, while slang refers to words and expressions used in <u>extremely</u> informal conversation and writing. Nonstandard language is quite common in popular music ("Uptight and Outta Sight," "You Turn Me On," "Mellow Yellow," "Ain't No Woman," "Dig").

REPETITION

Repetition helps the listener remember the title and/or the hook ("Monday, Monday," "Doctor! Doctor!," "Turn, Turn, Turn").

ALLUSION

An *allusion* is an indirect or casual reference to a well-known person, place or thing ("Kid Charlemagne"). Allusions are often made to literary sources, movies, television shows, advertisements, and songs ("The Ten Commandments of Love," "Lil' Red Riding Hood").

CLICHES

Familiar, worn-out phrases that have been overused in literature and conversation are known as *cliches*. *Believe it or not,* cliches often make effective song titles ("Easier Said Than Done," "Pride and Joy").

ADAGE/PROVERB

An *adage* or *proverb* is a familiar saying that is laced with wisdom or special meaning. Adages have long been put to effective use in songwriting ("Heart of Gold," "Heart of Stone," "Blue Skies").

ALTERED ADAGE

The *altered adage* is also called a *twist of phrase.* ("Love at First Sting," "Two Hearts are Better Than One," "Every Little Bit Hurts"). The altered adage gives new meaning to a traditional phrase.

ALLITERATION/ASSONANCE

Alliteration is the repetition of the same consonant sound ("I Feel Fine," "Blue Bayou," "We Gotta Get Out of This Place"). *Assonance* is the repetition of vowel sounds ("Ain't Got No Home," "Only the Lonely," "Blue Moon"). These techniques can be used to create catchy, memorable titles and lyrics.

PROSODY

Prosody is the art of matching the lyrics to the music in a naturally expressive manner. First of all, it is very important to see that the lyrics are accented properly. Song lyrics should be accented the same way they would be in a conversation, otherwise there is a distortion in meaning. Also, the lyrics should fit emotionally with the direction of the melodic line: for example, the word "falling" fits a descending melody, while the word "climbing" goes with an ascending melody. Be sure your lyrics and melody are on the same track emotionally (chords also influence the mood of the lyrics), and use appropriate accents.

IMAGES

Images—also called *picture words*—are vivid descriptions that help the listener actually visualize the person, place or object that is being described. The songs "Gentle on My Mind" and "Both Sides Now" are loaded with picture words. "The Star Spangled Banner" is another song with many dramatic images:

"dawn's early light"

"twilight's last gleaming"

"broad stripes and bright stars"

"rockets' red glare"

"bombs bursting in air"

WORDS - OR MUSIC - FIRST?

Aspiring songwriters often wonder if there is a correct order or procedure for writing songs. Some feel that perhaps the lyrics should be completed before the music is written; others think that maybe it is the other way around. Because professional songwriters have achieved success with both methods, it cannot be said that one approach is better than the other. In fact, some songwriters actually specialize in lyrics, while others work exclusively with music.

Some writers feel that it is confining to try to "fit" new lyrics with a pre-written melody (and vice versa), so another option is to write the words and music at the same time. This approach lets the writer match the lyrics with the melody "on the spot" and make modifications in phrasing, lyrics, and melodic contours as the work proceeds.

The best thing to do is to try various approaches and find the one that enables you to turn out your best work. Work habits vary, and each writer must discover his or her own strengths through experimentation.

CHECKLIST FOR TITLES, THEMES AND LYRICS

Before you consider your song to be finished, go through this checklist and analyze your work as closely as possible. The goal is to eliminate the weak spots that keep songs from reaching their full potential.

1. Does the title reveal something about the storyline?

2. Are the lyrics clear and easy to understand? Do they flow naturally?

3. Will the average listener find meaning in the lyrics?

4. Does the central theme come into focus early in the song?

5. Is the theme developed logically as the song proceeds?

6. Are the rhymes as strong as possible?

7. Does the beat of the music—and the melody—fit the mood of the lyrics?

8. Is the time-frame logical?

9. Is there a good hook, with enough repetition so that the listener will remember the hook?

10. Does each line have meaning, or are there non-essential lyrics that should be revised or eliminated?

11. Does your storyline contain conflicts that are brought to a satisfactory resolution?

12. If you aspire to write for the pop market, are you considering commercial music realities such as maximum time for airplay, contemporary trends, and so on?

SUGGESTED PROJECTS

1. Make a list of several of your favorite songs, and try to answer the following questions about each song:

   A) What is the central theme of this song?
   B) Are there any sub-themes?
   C) Is the title related to the central theme?
   D) What conflicts exist in the storyline? Are the conflicts ultimately resolved?
   E) Does this song make use of figurative language?
   F) What types of rhyming techniques are used in this song?
   G) What point of view is used to tell this song's story?

2. Use one or more of the techniques taught in this chapter to improve one of your original lyrics that needs polishing.

3. Read any poem of your own choice, and try to identify the use of any literary techniques you have learned in this chapter.

4

MELODY

The melody is the "tune" of the song that can be sung, hummed, or whistled. Many people are able to recall a song's melody long after they have forgotten the words and the recording artist.

This chapter teaches a number of techniques fundamental to the creation of an interesting melody. In addition, a number of scales are presented here, each accompanied by a melodic example. As you absorb the songwriting techniques and the scales into your musical vocabulary, you will find that your original melodies sound more professional than ever.

THE MOTIF

A melodic *motif* (also called a *motive*) is a short, recognizable fragment of a larger musical unit known as a *phrase*.* To keep things simple for now, let's call Ex. 1 a phrase and Ex. 2 a motif. Note that the music is similar to the tune "Shenandoah."

*Technically speaking, a phrase is usually two measures or more in length (see "Come All Ye Fair and Tender Ladies" on the next page for an example of this).

VARIATIONS ON THE MOTIF

Motives may be varied to create melodic ideas. The following examples, based on the motif above, demonstrate several ways to vary motives.

A) *Change the timing of the motif:*

B) *Change the time signature:*

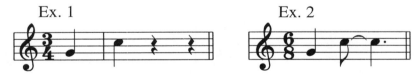

C) *Repeat one or more notes:*

D) *Substitute a new note in place of an original note:*

E) *Reverse the order of the notes:*

F) Another way to vary a motif is to *place the notes in every possible order*. To demonstrate this, we will use the four-note motif at the beginning of "Come All Ye Fair and Tender Ladies":

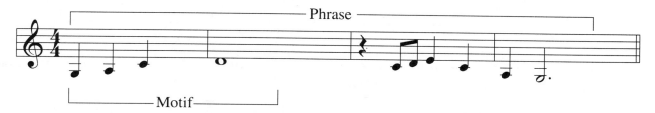

Placing the notes in every possible order yields 24 combinations:

1. GACD	7. AGCD	13. CGAD	19. DGAC
2. GADC	8. AGDC	14. CGDA	20. DGCA
3. GCAD	9. ACGD	15. CAGD	21. DAGC
4. GCDA	10. ACDG	16. CADG	22. DCGA
5. GDAC	11. ADGC	17. CDGA	23. DACG
6. GDCA	12. ADCG	18. CDAG	24. DCAG

By applying variations A - E to these note combinations, you can create literally hundreds of motives! Then, sort out the best ideas and incorporate them in your melody writing. Experimenting with the motives in this way is lots of fun, and it will give you a terrific feel for creating original music!

HOW TO CREATE MELODIES FROM MOTIVES AND PHRASES

A melody is a sequence of tones that is pleasant to the ear. We will now analyze several folk and blues song melodies to see how to create melodies from motives and phrases.

A) *Exact repetition* ("Brahm's Lullaby"):

Use exact repetition judiciously; overused, it can become monotonous.

B) *Sequential repetition* transfers the phrase (or motif) to another level of pitch. Each repetition is based on the same intervals as the original idea. For example, the arrangement of intervals in each of the three phrases of "Hava Nagilah" is unison – up a third – down a second – down a second:

51

C) An idea that is transferred to another pitch level may *keep the same melodic contour* or shape without necessarily having the same arrangement of intervals ("Hush Little Baby"):

D) A *melodically modified repetition* uses one or more new notes in place of an original note or notes, as shown in the first three phrases of "Tom Dooley":

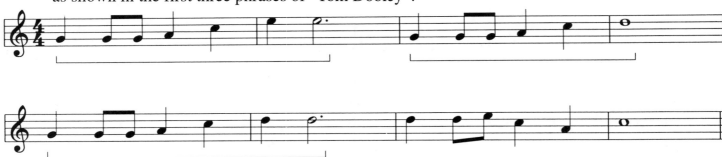

E) A *rhythmically modified repetition* reiterates the same notes, but with the rhythm of one or more notes altered:

F) "Sinner Man" begins with two distinct motives. The first motive is varied with sequential repetition (see ex. B above). The second motive is varied with sequential repetition *and* melodic modification; this technique is called a *combined sequential and modified* variation:

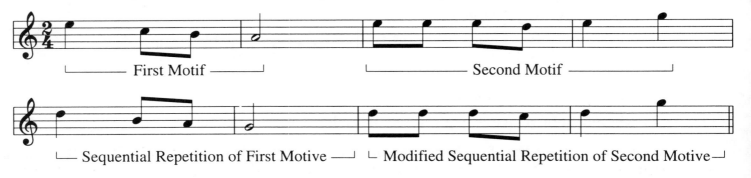

G) The second phrase of "Careless Love" shows how to *keep the rhythm of the initial phrase while varying the melody*:

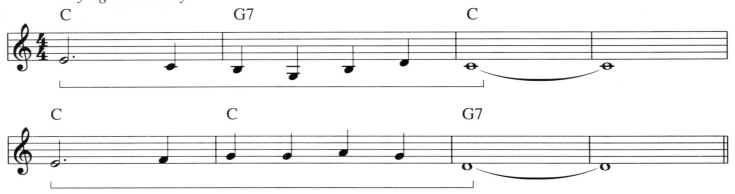

52

MORE METHODS FOR CREATING MELODIES

A. Play (or sing) a phrase, then answer back with a *contrasting phrase* ("Cripple Creek"):

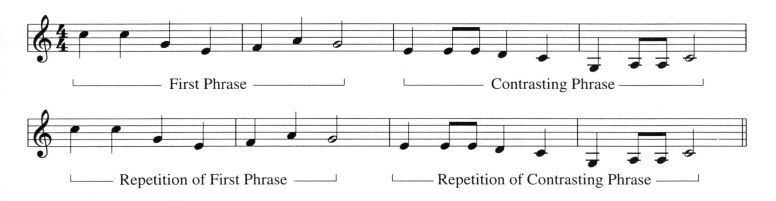

Contrast is also used in other ways. The first three phrases of "Tom Dooley" (p. 52) are quite similar; then, the verse is concluded with a fourth, contrasting phrase.

B. The chorus of "Let My People Go" uses *chord tones only* (also see the first three measures of "Careless Love," p. 52):

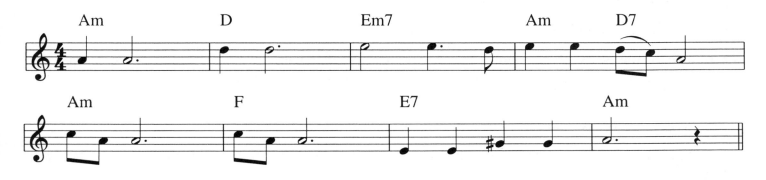

C. Melodies may also be based on *arpeggios* ("Red Wing"):

GUIDELINES FOR CREATING AND DEVELOPING MELODIES

1. Most melodies consist of stepwise motion (half-step and whole-step intervals), with larger intervals mixed in for variety.

2. Leaps (large intervals), which must be used sparingly, are usually followed by a series of descending pitches.

3. Commercial writing calls for melodies that are "catchy," with much repetition. Still, even commercial tunes must offer the listener some degree of contrast.

4. A good melody is characterized by variety: If there are a lot of notes in one phrase or section, the next phrase or section should be less active. When the music builds up to a high point of tension, relaxation should follow. Markedly dynamic areas of the music should be contrasted with a section that places less emphasis on dynamics.

5. Vary the length of the melodic phrases, but not to the extent that the natural metrical pattern is disrupted.

6. Do not have everything busy at the same time. A busy melody does not need as many chord changes as a less active melody.

7. Melodies written for singing must take the range of the vocalist into consideration (see page 57).

8. Keep the melody confined to just a few basic note values; using too many note values makes the melody sound choppy and forced.

9. Reverse the direction of the melodic line after every four or five notes.

10. Start the melody with an opening motif or phrase, and then vary the idea. Basic ideas can be varied with a number of techniques including rhythmic variation, repetition, melodic variation, contrast, and development (see examples on pages 51–53).

11. *Originality* is essential.

12. Do not be afraid to rewrite, edit, alter—or even start over—if doing so will make your song better.

BASIC SCALES FOR MELODIES

Listed here are several of the most common scales, each followed by a melodic example. The examples are in C (or C minor), and they may be transposed to any other key. The techniques for creating melodies, taught on the previous pages, may be applied to any of these scales.

1) MAJOR SCALE   C - D - E - F - G - A - B - C

Melody example from "The Cruel War" in the C *major scale:*

2) MAJOR PENTATONIC SCALE   C - D - E - G - A - C

Melody example: "The Midnight Special" in the C *major pentatonic scale:*

3) "RAGTIME" OR "MAJOR BLUES" SCALE   C - D - D♯ - E - G - A - C

You can use the *ragtime scale* in "Midnight Special" (above) by substituting the following notes for the notes in measures one and seven:

4) NATURAL MINOR SCALE   C - D - E♭ - F - G - A♭ - B♭ - C

Melody example: "Reflections" (Mendelssohn) in C *natural minor:*

5) MINOR PENTATONIC SCALE   C - E♭ - F - G - B♭ - C

There is no key signature for the *minor pentatonic scale*. Here, the accidentals are applied as needed.
Melody example: "Bluemood" in the *C minor pentatonic scale:*

6) BLUES SCALE   C - E♭ - F - F♯ - G - B♭ - C

The *blues scale* is also called the *minor blues scale*. This scale can be used in "Bluemood" (above) by
changing the last bar to this:

7) DORIAN (DORIAN MINOR) SCALE   C - D - E♭ - F - G - A - B♭ - C

Melodies in the *dorian minor scale* are said to be in the *dorian mode*. When an entire song is based on
this scale, the words Dorian Mode may appear above the key signature.

Melody example: "Scarborough Fair" in C dorian:

C Dorian

8) **MAJOR HEXATONIC SCALE**   C - D - E - F - G - A - C

This *major hexatonic scale* is a major scale minus its seventh tone. No special key signature is required for this scale.

Melody example: "Sally Goodin'" in the C major hexatonic scale:

9)   **MINOR HEXATONIC SCALE**   C - D - E♭ - F - G - B♭ - C

The *minor hexatonic scale* is also known as the *minor six-tone scale*. Songs using this scale take the natural minor key signature, even though the melody omits the sixth.

Melody example: "Shady Grove" in the C minor hexatonic scale:

VOCAL RANGE

Needless to say, not all singers have the same vocal range. Be sure that your melody will not strain the ability of the vocalist it is intended for. The average singer (including most rock singers) will have a range of an octave or less (see comparison chart, below). Many semipro and professional singers can sing up to an octave plus a fifth, but only above average to exceptional vocalists have a range of a thirteenth or more.

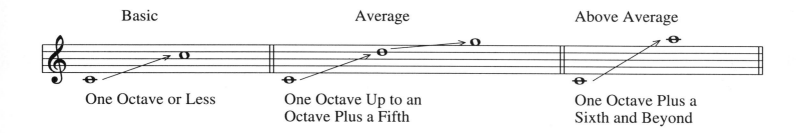

SUGGESTED PROJECTS

1. Identify the opening motif (three notes or more) in any song (or songs) of your own choice.

2. Vary this motif using the following methods:

    A) Change the timing
    B) Change the time signature
    C) Repeat one or more notes
    D) Substitute a new note for an original note
    E) Reverse the order of the notes
    F) Place the notes in every possible order

3. Apply the following variations to any motif or phrase of your choice:

    A) Sequential repetition
    B) Keep the same melodic contour
    C) Melodically modified repetition
    D) Rhythmically modified repetition
    E) Combined sequential and modified repetition
    F) Keep the rhythm, vary the melody

4. Listen to several recordings of your favorite singer. Transcribe the vocal part of each recording, and assess the range of the singer.

5. Using any of the scales taught in this chapter, write an original melody in a scale you have not used before.

5

CHORDS

The melodies and harmonies in any given major key are based on the corresponding major scale. Every major key has a harmonic foundation of seven chords, each built on a tone from the scale. The chords add an emotional quality to the music that complements and enhances the melody line.

This chapter teaches the fundamentals of chord construction (how chords are derived from scales) and harmonic application (how chords work). By mastering these fundamentals you will become more versatile and creative, and your music will sound more professional than ever.

TRIADS

The simplest chords contain only three notes and are called *triads*. There are four basic *types* of triads: major, minor, augmented, and diminished. The notes in each chord may be found by applying the appropriate *chord formula* to the corresponding major scale. A chord formula is a group of numbers that indicates which scale tones should be combined to make up a given chord.

MAJOR TRIAD

A major triad is notated by the name of its root tone only; for example, a C major triad is notated as C, a B♭ major triad is notated as B♭, and so on. In conversation, musicians refer to major triads by their root tone only, so a C major triad is simply called a C chord. All other *chord types* have additional descriptive information attached to the name of their root tone (Cm7, D9, etc.).

The *chord tones* in each major triad may be found by locating the first, third, and fifth tones in the corresponding major scale. For example, the C chord is made up of the first, third, and fifth tones of the C major scale.

Result: The C chord contains the notes C- E- G, the 1-3-5 tones of the scale. Technically speaking, the notes in any chord may be played in any conceivable order or combination. Note, for instance, that the basic "C" chord on the guitar is made up of two C notes, two E notes, and one G note.

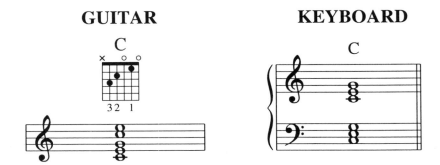

To find the notes in the G chord, simply pick out the 1 - 3 - 5 tones of the G major scale (p. 63), G- B- D. It's easy! The notes in the F chord are F - A - C, and so on.

TERMS: "FORMULA" AND "SPELLING"

The group of numbers indicating the tones in a given chord type is known as the chord *formula*. Thus, the formula for any major triad is 1-3-5.

The group of tones that make up a given chord is known as the chord *spelling*. Thus, the spelling for the C major triad is C-E-G.

MINOR TRIAD

The formula for the *minor triad*, written Cmi or Cm, is 1-♭3-5. The ♭3 (flatted third) tone results from lowering the third scale tone by a half-step. Therefore, the Cm chord contains the notes C-E♭-G. What are the notes in Gm? (Hint: locate the first, flatted third, and fifth tones in the G major scale to find the notes in Gm*).

GUITAR
Cm

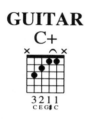

KEYBOARD
Cm

AUGMENTED TRIAD

* Answer: Gm = G - B♭ - D, or 1 - ♭3 - 5 of the G major scale.

The *augmented triad* formula is 1 - 3 - ♯5. The ♯5 ("sharped fifth" or "sharp five") tone results from raising the fith scale tone by a half-step. Therefore, C augmented (Caug or C+) is spelled C - E - G♯.

KEYBOARD
C+

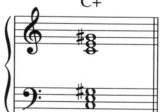

GUITAR
C+

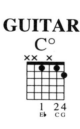

DIMINISHED TRIAD

The *diminished triad* (C°) formula is 1 -♭3-♭5, so C° is C, E♭, G♭. This chord is also called "minor, flat 5" (Cm♭5).

GUITAR
C°

KEYBOARD
C°

Try to build each of the above chord types on several root tones, referring to the major scale table (p. 63) as needed.

Table 2: Summary of the four basic triads

TYPE	FORMULA	EXAMPLE IN G
Major triad	1 - 3 - 5	G - B - D
Minor triad	1 - ♭3 - 5	G - B♭ - D
Augmented triad	1 - 3 - ♯5	G - B - D♯
Diminished triad	1 - ♭3 - ♭5	G - B♭ - D♭

DIATONIC TRIADS IN C

The harmonic (chordal) foundation of each key is a series of seven simple three-note chords (triads). Each triad is built on a scale tone. Here are the triads in the key of C, and the tones in each triad:

Triads in C:	C	Dm	Em	F	G	Am	Bm♭5
Chord tones:	C-E-G	D-F-A	E-G-B	F-A-C	G-B-D	A-C-E	B-D-F

KEYBOARD CHORDS

GUITAR CHORDS

The seven basic triads are called *diatonic* triads, meaning "in the key." The diatonic triads are the most basic chords in any key, and many simple songs contain only diatonic chords.

HOW TO BUILD DIATONIC TRIADS FROM DIATONIC SCALE TONES

We will now learn an easy way to build the diatonic triads in C from the C major scale tones. First, let's write out the notes in the C scale to cover two octaves:

C - D - E - F - G - A - B - C - D - E - F - G - A - B - C

1. For the first chord, start with the first letter: C

2. Skip a letter (D) and choose the next letter: E

3. Skip the next letter (F) and choose the following letter: G

This method gives us the notes (C-E-G) that make up the C chord. Being the first chord, C is known as the *tonic chord*. (Likewise, the G chord is the tonic chord in the key of G, the D chord is the tonic chord in the key of D, and so on.)

To find the notes in the second chord, Dm, follow this procedure:

1. Start with the letter D
2. Skip a letter (E) and choose the next letter: F
3. Skip the next letter (G) and choose the following letter: A

The result is Dm = D-F-A. The notes in the other diatonic chords may be found by following the same procedure. Start on any root tone and think: *keep* - skip - *keep* - skip - *keep*. You can find the triads in any major key by applying this technique to the corresponding scale.

Table 3: The major scales

NAME	SCALE TONES	NAME	SCALE TONES
B♭	B♭ - C - D - E♭ - F - G - A - B♭	B	B - C♯ - D♯ - E - F♯ - G♯ - A♯ - B
F	F - G - A - B♭ - C - D - E - F	F♯	F♯ - G♯ - A♯ - B - C♯ - D♯ - E♯ - F♯
C	C - D - E - F - G - A - B - C	G♭	G♭ - A♭ - B♭ - C♭ - D♭ - E♭ - F - G♭
G	G - A - B - C - D - E - F♯ - G	C♯	C♯ - D♯ - E♯ - F♯ - G♯ - A♯ - B♯ - C♯
D	D - E - F♯ - G - A - B - C♯ - D	D♭	D♭ - E♭ - F - G♭ - A♭ - B♭ - C - D♭
A	A - B - C♯ - D - E - F♯ - G♯ - A	A♭	A♭ - B♭ - C - D♭ - E♭ - F - G - A♭
E	E - F♯ - G♯ - A - B - C♯ - D♯ - E	E♭	E♭ - F - G - A♭ - B♭ - C - D - E♭

Table 4: Diatonic triads in seven keys

KEY		DIATONIC TRIADS					
B♭	**B♭**	**Cm**	**Dm**	**E♭**	**F**	**Gm**	**Am♭5**
	B♭-D-F	C-E♭-G	D-F-A	E♭-G-B♭	F-A-C	G-B♭-D	A-C-E♭
F	**F**	**Gm**	**Am**	**B♭**	**C**	**Dm**	**Em♭5**
	F-A-C	G-B♭-D	A-C-E	B♭-D-F	C-E-G	D-F-A	E-G-B♭
C	**C**	**Dm**	**Em**	**F**	**G**	**Am**	**Bm♭5**
	C-E-G	D-F-A	E-G-B	F-A-C	G-B-D	A-C-E	B-D-F
G	**G**	**Am**	**Bm**	**C**	**D**	**Em**	**F♯m♭5**
	G-B-D	A-C-E	B-D-F♯	C-E-G	D-F♯-A	E-G-B	F♯-A-C
D	**D**	**Em**	**F♯m**	**G**	**A**	**Bm**	**C♯m♭5**
	D-F♯-A	E-G-B	F♯-A-C♯	G-B-D	A-C♯-E	B-D-F♯	C♯-E-G
A	**A**	**Bm**	**C♯m**	**D**	**E**	**F♯m**	**G♯m♭5**
	A-C♯-E	B-D-F♯	C♯-E-G♯	D-F♯-A	E-G♯-B	F♯-A-C♯	G♯-B-D
E	**E**	**F♯m**	**G♯m**	**A**	**B**	**C♯m**	**D♯m♭5**
	E-G♯-B	F♯-A-C♯	G♯-B-D♯	A-C♯-E	B-D♯-F♯	C♯-E-G♯	D♯-F♯-A
	I	iim	iiim	IV	V	vim	viim♭5

ROMAN NUMERALS

At the bottom of Table Four (previous page) are seven Roman numerals which are used to identify each chord by scale position and type (major, minor, etc.). Note that the triads built on the first, fourth, and fifth tones are major (I, IV, V); the triads built on the second, third, and sixth tones are minor (iim, iiim, vim); and the triad built on the seventh tone is minor flat five (viim♭5). The minor flat five, also called a diminished triad, is rarely used in actual practice. Consequently, the "most important" basic triads in each major key are the I, iim, iiim, IV, V, and vim chords.

TRANSPOSING WITH ROMAN NUMERALS

The Roman numeral system allows us to 1) *transpose* chord progressions from one key to another, and 2) better identify aural relationships between chords.

Here is a typical chord progression in C:

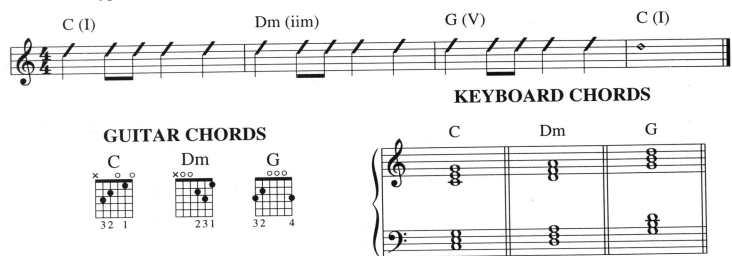

Now let's transpose the chord progression to G by finding the I, iim, and V chords in G:

See how easy it is to transpose with Roman numerals?

PRIMARY CHORDS I-IV-V

The I, IV, and V chords (in any key) are known as the *primary chords*. Thus, the primary chords in the key of C are C (I), F (IV), and G (V).

BASIC CHORD PROGRESSIONS WITH PRIMARY CHORDS

I-V

Some songs, such as "Land of 1,000 Dances," use only the I chord throughout the entire song. Others, including "Jambalaya," "Paperback Writer," and "Waltz Across Texas," use only I and V. "By the Light of the Moon" is another song that contains only the I and V chords. When you play the chords to the melody of "By the Light of the Moon," you will hear the relationship between the I and V chords.

By The Light Of The Moon

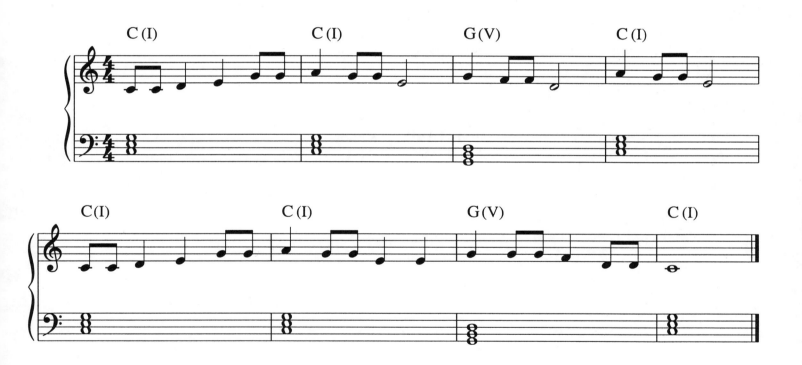

GUITAR CHORDS

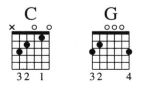

Note that I and V create a strong key feeling. This is because V is a place of "tension" and I is a place of "rest." Another way to put it is that "V likes to go to I" in order to produce a smooth resolution from a point of tension to a place of rest.

Keyboard voicings

1. Because of the fundamental nature of this book, most of the keyboard voicings are in root position.

2. Teachers may wish to advise beginners that the G chord in "By the Light of the Moon" is normally played an octave higher than written. However, writing the chord in the lower octave makes it convenient for the instructor to teach chord inversion (see example):

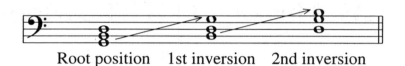

Root position   1st inversion   2nd inversion

This method of notation is used whenever possible throughout this chapter.

I-IV-V

Songs that use only the primary chords I-IV-V are known as *trichordal* songs. There are literally thousands of I-IV-V songs; examples include "Twist and Shout," "Wildwood Flower," and "Big Boss Man."

Wildwood Flower

Technically, the term "trichordal" is not restricted to I-IV-V (although that is what it usually refers to). For example, Bob Dylan's "You Ain't Goin' Nowhere" is a trichordal song that uses only the I, iim, and IV chords.

SECONDARY CHORDS

The iim, iiim, vim, and viim♭5 chords are called *secondary chords*. Of these chords, the iim, iiim, and vim are used most often. We will now study some typical chord progressions made up of primary *and* secondary chords:

I - vim - iim - V

The I-vim-iim-V progression is found in countless tunes including "Blue Moon," "This Boy," and "Molly Malone."

Molly Malone

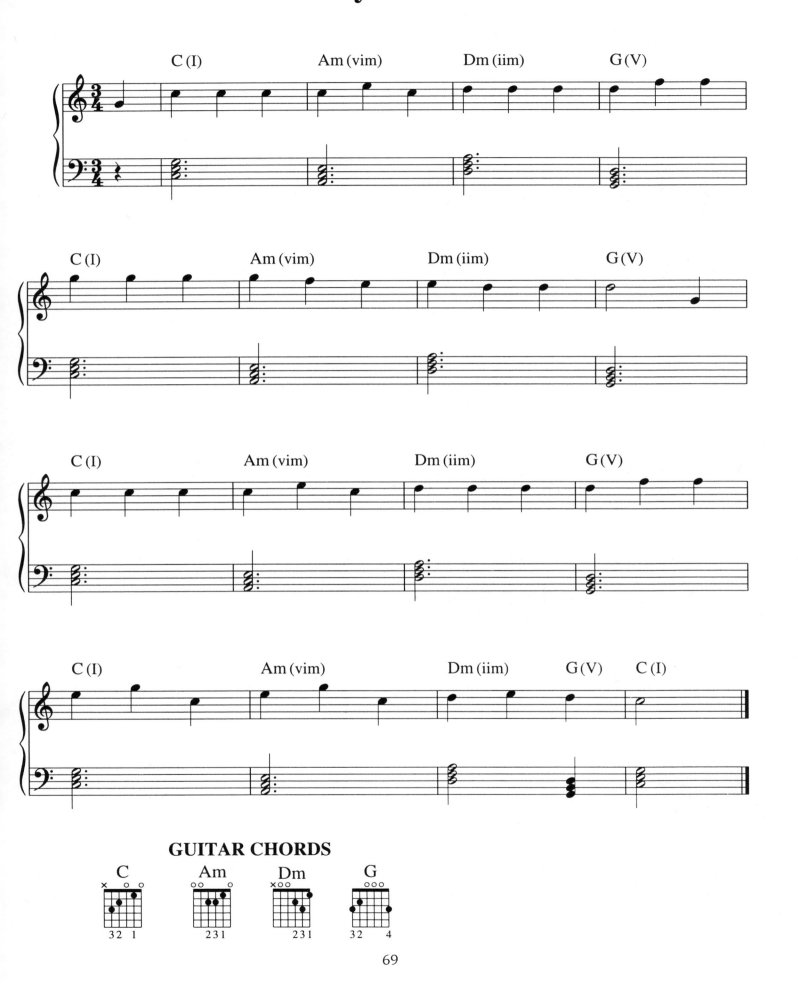

I- vim - IV - V and iim - V - I

The I-vim-IV-V chord progression is a variation on I-vim-iim-V. Both progressions are contained in the following arrangement of "Swing Low, Sweet Chariot." Another important progression appearing here is iim-V-I.

Swing Low, Sweet Chariot

GUITAR CHORDS

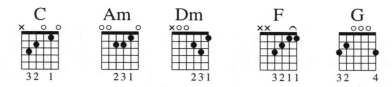

I - iiim - iim - V and iiim - iim - V - I

Measures five through eight of "Sloop John B." contains the I - iiim - iim - V chord progression; the iiim - iim - V - I progression is located in measures six through nine. We could also analyze measures five through nine as follows: I - iiim - iim - V - I. All are standard diatonic chord progressions found in all popular musical styles. The non-diatonic ivm chord (mes. 12) is discussed on page 83.

Sloop John B.

FOUR-NOTE CHORDS

Triads are fine for simple music, but modern musical sounds are created with chords that contain four or more notes. We will now learn to build four types of *seventh chords*, and also the *major sixth chord*. The seventh chords and the major sixth chords are made up of four notes.

MAJOR SEVENTH CHORD

Symbol: Cmaj7 (CM7, CMA7, C△7)
Formula: 1 - 3- 5 - 7
Spelling: C - E- G - B

MINOR SEVENTH CHORD

Symbol: Cm7 (Cmi7, C⁻7)
Formula: 1-♭3- 5- ♭7
Spelling: C - E♭ - G- B♭

DOMINANT SEVENTH CHORD

Symbol: C7
Formula: 1- 3- 5 - ♭7
Spelling: C - E - G - B♭

DIMINISHED SEVENTH CHORD

Symbol: C°7 (Cdim7)
Formula: 1-♭3-♭5 - ♭♭7 (1 - ♭3 - ♭5 - 6)
Spelling: C - E♭ - G♭ - B♭♭ (C - E♭ - G♭- A)

MAJOR SIXTH CHORD

Symbol: C6
Formula: 1- 3- 5 - 6
Spelling: C - E - G - A

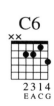

DIATONIC SEVENTH CHORDS

We will now learn about the four-note, key-related chords called *diatonic seventh chords*. Let's start by writing out our two-octave C scale:

C - D - E - F - G - A - B - C - D - E - F - G - A - B - C

Remember, the basic C triad = CEG. To get a four-note C chord, simply skip the note which follows G (A), and go on to B. Add B to the C-E-G and you have C-E-G-B (1 -3 -5 - 7). This chord is called C major seven, and it is written CMAJ7, or CM7, or CMA7. Here are the seventh chords in the key of C:

IMAJ7	iim7	iiim7	IVMAJ7	V7	vim7	viim7♭5
CMAJ7	Dm7	Em7	FMAJ7	G7	Am7	Bm7♭5
C-E-G-B	D-F-A-C	E-G-B-D	F-A-C-E	G-B-D-F	A-C-E-G	B-D-F-A

KEYBOARD CHORDS

GUITAR CHORDS

The diatonic seventh chords fall in the following categories or types:

I MAJ7 and IVMAJ7 are major seventh chords (1-3-5-7).

iim7, iiim7 and vim7 are minor seventh chords (1-♭3-5-♭7).

V7 is a dominant seventh chord (1-3-5-♭7).

viim♭5 is a "minor seven flat-five chord," also called "half-diminished" (1-♭3-♭5-♭7). The symbol for half-diminished is ø, so Bm7♭5 may also be labeled Bø .

The seventh chords have a richer, more modern sound than the plain triads. To learn the sound of them, play the following song, "Seventh Avenue." For best results, learn some other tunes that use diatonic seventh chords, and be sure to work in a variety of keys.

Seventh Avenue

L. McCabe

Relaxed swing

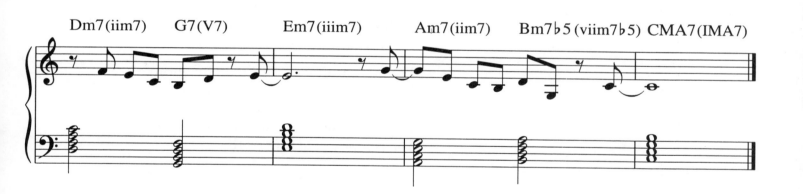

GUITAR CHORDS

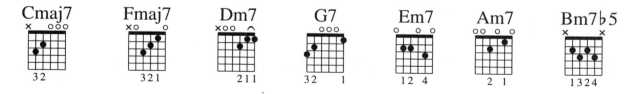

V CAN BE V7

In almost all songs, the V7 may be played instead of V. Therefore, G7 may replace the plain G chord in the key of C, D7 may replace the plain D chord in the key of G, and so on. Try playing the songs on pages 65, 67, 69, 70, and 72 with V7 instead of V.

Table 5: Basic functions of the diatonic chords

CHORD	EXAMPLES IN C	BASIC FUNCTIONS
I MAJOR	C, C6, CMAJ7	1) Tonic chord – place of rest 2) May move to any other chord 3) Often follows V or V7
iim	Dm, Dm7	1) Subdominant function (tends to move to V7) 2) Can substitute for IV 3) Often follows vim or VI7
iiim	Em, Em7	1) May substitute for I (tonic function) 2) Sometimes follows V7 3) Often moves to vim or VI7 4) May move to VII7
IVMAJOR	F, F6, FMAJ7	1) Subdominant function (tends to move to V7) 2) Also moves to I, II7, and ivm
V Dominant	G7 (or G triad)	1) Dominant function (tends to move to I) 2) Sometimes moves to a subdominant (iim or IV) 3) Sometimes moves to II7 or iiim
vim	Am, Am7	1) May substitute for I (tonic function) 2) Frequently follows I or iiim 3) Often moves to iim or II7 4) Is often placed between iiim (or III7) and iim 5) Also moves to iiim or III7
viim♭5	Bm♭5, Bm7♭5	1) May substitute for V7 (dominant function) 2) Usually moves up a fourth in the bass to a minor or dom.7 chord (ex: Bm7♭5 moves to Em7 or E7)

2-5-1

Another way to analyze chord movement is to recognize that a great deal of chord movement follows this pattern:

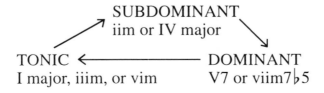

SUBDOMINANT
iim or IV major

TONIC ← DOMINANT
I major, iiim, or vim   V7 or viim7♭5

"Satin Doll" by Duke Ellington is a classic example of "2-5-1" chord movement.

CADENCES

Certain chord progressions known as *chord cadences* often occur at the end of musical phrases. Here we will discuss the cadences involving the I, IV, V7, and vim chords.

PERFECT CADENCE

The *perfect cadence* occurs when V (or V7) moves to I. This cadence, also known as a *full close*, takes the harmony from a point of tension (V or V7) to a place of rest (I). We will use the ending of "Sloop John B." to demonstrate the perfect cadence.

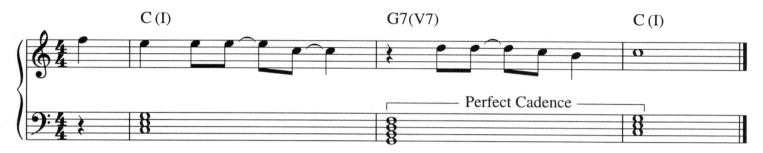

GUITAR CHORDS

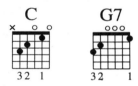

The entire song "Sloop John B." appears on page 72.

PLAGAL CADENCE

IV moving to I is called the *plagal cadence*. This chord change brings the harmony "home," but with less force than the V-I change. Because the plagal cadence is often used at the end of hymns, it is also called the *Amen cadence*. The ending of "Mountains of Mourne" is used to demonstrate the plagal cadence.

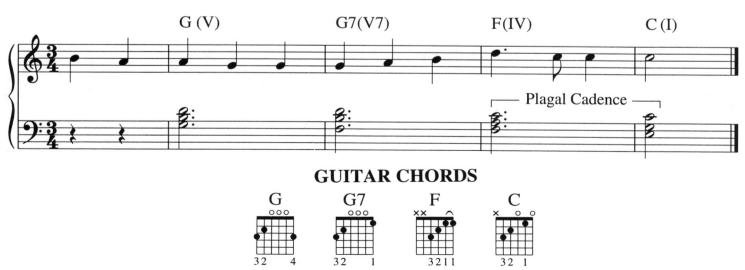

GUITAR CHORDS

"Mountains of Mourne" appears in its entirety on page 81.

IMPERFECT CADENCE

The *imperfect cadence*—also called a *half close*—takes place when either I, IV, or vim progresses to V (or V7).* Because of the tension created by the V (or V7) chord, the imperfect cadence sounds like it "wants to continue." The most common placement of this cadence is at the end of a phrase other than the final phrase or ending. (See the end of phrases two and three of "The Riddle Song" below.) In rare circumstances, the imperfect cadence is used to create an unusual, unresolved ending, as demonstrated in the following arrangement of "The Riddle Song."

*I to IV is also called an imperfect cadence.

The Riddle Song

GUITAR CHORDS

78

DECEPTIVE CADENCE

When the V (or V7) chord moves to vim—or to any chord other than I—we have a *deceptive cadence* (also called the *interrupted cadence*). Because the ear expects V (V7) to go to I (especially in the final phrase), the deceptive cadence adds an element of surprise to the harmonic progression. The next example shows how bluegrass players often end the instrumental "Blackberry Blossom" on a deceptive cadence. For a change of pace, this example is in the key of G.

GUITAR CHORDS

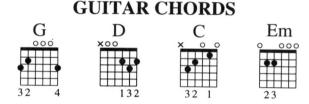

NON-DIATONIC CHORDS

Any chord with one or more notes outside the corresponding major scale is a *non-diatonic* chord. For example, the E7 chord (E-G♯-B-D) is non-diatonic to the key of C because the G♯ note is not in the C major scale. When properly handled, non-diatonic chords add a nice touch of color to chord progressions. Compare the following example to measures 4-8 of "Molly Malone" on page 69.

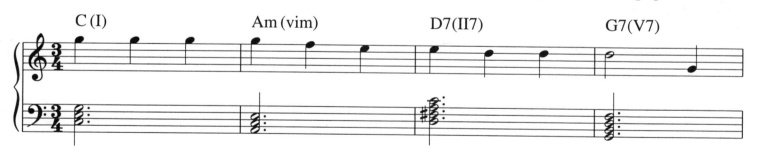

GUITAR CHORDS

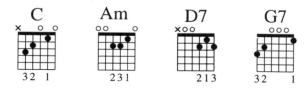

Note that the non-diatonic chord D7 (II7) has been substituted for the diatonic Dm (iim) to add more color to the progression. Technically, the II7 is in a category of chords known as secondary dominant chords.

SECONDARY DOMINANT CHORDS

A *secondary dominant chord* is a dominant seventh-type chord built on any scale tone other than the fifth scale tone:

Secondary dominant chords in C:

C7 (I7)	D7 (II7)	E7 (III7)	F7 (IV7)	A7 (VI7)	B7 (VII7)
C-E-G-B♭	D-F♯-A-C	E-G♯-B-D	F-A-C-E♭	A-C♯-E-G	B-D♯-F♯-A

"Mountains of Mourne" uses three secondary dominant chords—I7, II7, and VI7.

Mountains of Mourne

GUITAR CHORDS

"Secondary Sounds" uses four secondary dominant chords – VII7, III7, VI7, and II7:

Secondary Sounds

L. McCabe

GUITAR CHORDS

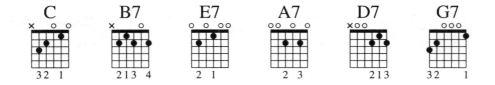

See "Backporch Blues" (p. 27), for a typical use of the IV7 chord. Note that each secondary dominant chord is a non-diatonic chord. The following table shows the most common functions of the secondary dominant chords.

Table 6: Basic functions of the secondary dominant chords

CHORD	EXAMPLES IN C	BASIC FUNCTIONS
I7	C7	1) Replaces I in the blues 2) Moves to IV (F) 3) Moves to IV7 (F7) in the blues 4) May also move to vim
II7	D7	1) Moves to V7 (G7) 2) Sometimes moves to iim (Dm)
III7	E7	1) Moves to vim (Am) 2) Moves to VI7 (A7) 3) Moves to IV (F)
IV7	F7	1) Replaces IV in the blues 2) Sometimes moves to ♭VII (B♭) 3) Might move to ♯IV°7 (F♯°7), then to I (C)
VI7	A7	1) Moves to II7 (D7) 2) Moves to iim (Dm)
VII7	B7	1) Moves to III7 (E7) 2) Moves to iiim (Em)

As you can see, the secondary dominant chords quite often move to another dominant chord—or to a minor chord—whose root is a perfect fourth above (or a perfect fifth below).

NON-DIATONIC MINOR CHORDS

Non-diatonic minor chords on im, ivm, or vm are used in almost every musical style. The ivm chord, which is used more often than im or vm, appears in "Sloop John B." (p. 72).

Table 7: Basic functions of non-diatonic minor chords im, ivm, vm

CHORD	EXAMPLES IN C	BASIC FUNCTIONS
im, im7	Cm, Cm7	Usually moves to V7 (G7), or IV7 (F7), or ♭VII7 (B♭7)
ivm, ivm7	Fm, Fm7	1) Most often moves to I 2) Often follows IV (IV-ivm-I) 3) Occurs between iim and I
vm, vm7	Gm, Gm7	The common vm7-I7-IV progression (Gm7-C7-F) is actually a modulation to F major (iim7-V7-I)

Another minor chord, the minor seven flat five (m7♭5), is diatonic only on the seventh scale degree (viim7♭5 = Bm7♭5). This type of chord often progresses up a perfect fourth to a dominant seven-type chord (C-F-Em7♭5-A7).

TERTIARY CHORDS

Sometimes the term *tertiary* is applied to chords built on non-diatonic tones; for example, the ♭II7 chord in the key of C (D♭7) is sometimes called a *tertiary dominant* chord.

THE SIX-CHORD ROCK SYSTEM

The major triads I, ♭III, IV, V, ♭VI, and ♭VII are frequently used – in various combinations – for rock chord progressions. In recent practice, the thirds have been omitted from the chords, leaving just the root and the fifth. Such chords may be labeled C5, G5, and so on. "Punk Rock Breakdown" will give you a basic feel for these chords in a rock setting.

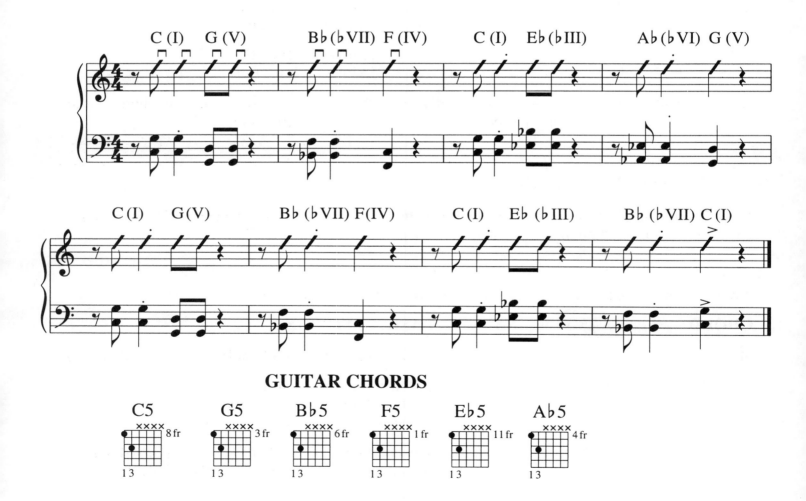

Punk Rock Breakdown

L. McCabe

DIMINISHED SEVENTH CHORD FUNCTION

The *diminished seventh chord* is a "tension" chord containing the $1 - \flat3 - \flat5 - 6$ tones; therefore, Cdim7 = C-E$\flat$- G$\flat$-A. The chord is also written C°7. Since the dim. 7 chord is built in minor thirds, any of its notes can be the root:

C-E$\flat$-G$\flat$-A = C°7	D$\flat$-E-G-B$\flat$ = D$\flat$°7	D-F-A$\flat$-B = D°7
E$\flat$-G$\flat$-A-C = E$\flat$°7	E-G-B$\flat$-C$\sharp$ = E°7	F-A$\flat$-B-D = F°7
G$\flat$-A-C-E$\flat$ = G$\flat$°7	G-B$\flat$-D$\flat$-E = G°7	A$\flat$-B-D-F = A$\flat$°7
A-C-E$\flat$-F$\sharp$ = A°7	B$\flat$-D$\flat$-E-G = B$\flat$°7	B-D-F-G$\sharp$ = B°7

There are only three dim. 7 chords, each having four possible names. Because the dim. 7 chord is not diatonic to any major key, it operates as a "passing chord." The most common function of the diminished chord is to connect two chords containing notes that are a whole step apart.

Example: C = C E G   Am = A C E

There is a whole step between the G note in the C chord and the A note in the Am chord. Therefore, we will add to our chord progression a diminished chord on the note in between the G and the A (G$\sharp$).

DIMINISHED CHORD: EXAMPLE ONE

Original Chord Progression
C   Am

New Chord Progression
C   G#°7   Am

GUITAR CHORDS

KEYBOARD CHORDS

A very obvious use of the diminished chord, then, would be to connect two chords whose roots are a whole step apart:

DIMINISHED CHORD: EXAMPLE TWO

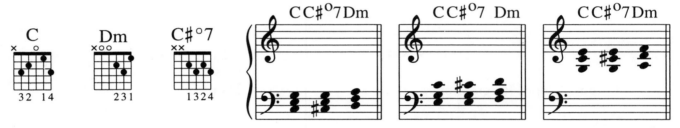

Original Chord Progression
C   Dm

New Chord Progression
C   C#°7   Dm

GUITAR CHORDS

C   Dm   C#°7
x   o   xoo   xx
32 14   231   1324

KEYBOARD CHORDS

C C#°7 Dm   C C#°7 Dm   C C#°7 Dm

The diminished triad provides the best voice-leading for this example. Try each of the three combinations shown above.

The addition of the diminished chord must be done with discretion, and should only be done when it enhances the melody.

The following example shows how C♯°7 chord could be substituted for C in "Mountains of Mourne" (p. 81) to improve the harmony.

"Mountains Of Mourne" With Diminished Chord

NEW CHORD

AUGMENTED CHORD FUNCTION

Like the diminished chord, the augmented triad (1 - 3 - ♯5) and the *dominant seventh augmented* (1 - 3 - ♯5 - ♭7) chords are "tension" chords that connect one chord to another. The symbol for C augmented is C aug or C+; the symbol for C augmented 7 is Caug7 or C7+. The *augmented chord* (triad or seventh chord) is also known as the "sharp five" chord.

Because the augmented triads are built in major thirds, there are four in all, each having three possible names:

C-E-G♯ = C+	D♭-F-A = D♭+
E-G♯-C = E+	F-A-C♯ = F+
A♭-C-E = A♭+	A-C♯-F = A+
D-F♯-A♯ = D+	E♭-G-B = E♭+
F♯-A♯-D = F♯+	G-B-D♯ = G+
B♭-D-F♯ = B♭+	B-D♯-G = B+

The most common function of the augmented chord (triad or seventh) is to connect a chord to another chord whose root is a perfect fourth above. This principle is demonstrated in the following arrangement of "Careless Love."

Careless Love

GUITAR CHORDS

ABOUT KEYBOARD VOICINGS

Keyboard teachers should explain how chord inversions may be used to create smooth voice-leading (mes. 10–13, etc.). Also, show beginners how to invert some of the root-position chords (G7 in mes 2, F in mes. 3, etc.) to produce better voice-leading.

CHORDS AND PROGRESSIONS IN "CARELESS LOVE"

A) I, iim, iiim, IV, V7, and vim

B) The "2-5-1" progression (mes. 7–9 and mes. 14–15)

C) The diminished chord in mes. 12 connects two chords having tones a whole step apart

F (F̲-A-C) → F♯°7 (F̲♯-A-C-E♭) → C(C-E-G̲)

D) The I - vim - iim - V7 progression (mes. 13-14)

E) I - I⁺ - IV (mes. 10–11)

Another standard use of the augmented chord is to connect a major (or dominant) chord to a minor chord whose root is three half-steps below. Always take care that the "sharp five" tone in the augmented chord does not clash with the written melody.

Another Augmented Connection

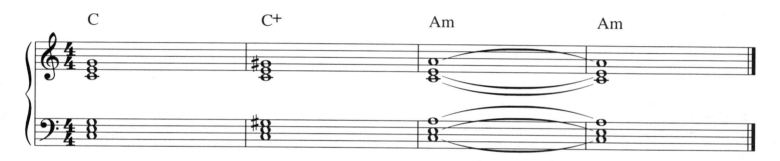

GUITAR CHORDS

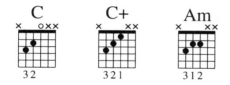

SUSPENDED CHORD FUNCTION

Suspended chords—also called *suspended fourth chords*—are very effective when a "wispy" or "airy" effect is desired:

NAME	FORMULA	TONES
C sus (C sus4)*	1-4-5	C-F-G
C7sus (C7sus4)*	1-4-5-♭7	C-F-G-B♭
Cm sus (Cm sus4)	1-♭3-4-5	C-E♭-F-G
Cm7sus(Cm7sus4)	1-♭3-4-5-♭7	C-E♭-F-G-B♭

* The third is always omitted from these chords

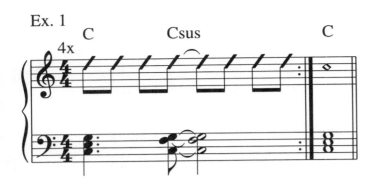

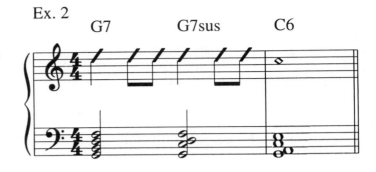

GUITAR CHORDS

GUITAR CHORDS

ROOT PROGRESSIONS

The following table contains nine root (or bass) progressions arranged from the strongest or most logical (top) to the weakest (bottom). Although there is no absolute agreement on an exact hierarchy of logical root progressions, this table is a good place to start. Intervals that are omitted from this table are considered to be weak in terms of bass movement.

Table 8: Root progressions arranged in order of strength

TYPE	EXAMPLE
1. Up a perfect fourth [a]	C - F
2. Down a half step	C - Bm
3. Up - or down - a whole step	C - Dm; C - B♭
4. Up a perfect fifth [b]	C - G7
5. Up a half step	C - D♭7
6. Up (or down) a major third	C - Em; C - A♭7
7. Up a major sixth [c]	C - A7
8. Up a minor third [d]	C - E♭°7
9. Up (or down) a tritone [e]	C - G♭

a. Same as down a perfect fifth. This is the strongest or most logical root progression.
b. Same as down a perfect fourth.
c. Same as down a minor third.
d. Same as down a major sixth.
e. A tritone – three whole tones – is the same going up or down.

SUGGESTED PROJECTS

1. Using a songbook for reference, find and analyze the use of each of the following chord types. Specifically, analyze the usage of each chord in relationship to its preceding and following chords as well as its function (position) in the key. Use Roman numerals for your analyses.

   A) Augmented triad

   B) Dominant seven sharp-five (augmented seventh)

   C) Diminished seventh chord (Note: this chord is often indicated as a diminished triad, e.g. C°).

   D) Suspended fourth chord

2. Using a songbook for reference, find and analyze the use of each of the secondary dominant chords:

   A) I7   B) II7   C) III7   D) IV7   E) VI7   F) VII7

3. Using Roman numerals, transpose the chord progression of any song to several other keys.

4. Try to locate a song which uses a IMAJ7 and/or a IVMAJ7. Analyze the melody and/or the "mood" of the music to determine why the major seventh sound "works" better than a plain triad.

5. Use the chords in the "six chord rock system" to compose an original chord progression. Select the key and song form of your own choice.

6

FINDING THE RIGHT CHORDS FOR THE MELODY

Because chords can add a great emotional dimension to songs, it is very important to find the right chords for your original melodies. The wrong chord in the wrong place will not only weaken a good melody, it may actually make a fine tune unsuitable for performance or recording. Here, we will cover the fundamentals of chord-melody relationships to help you find the right chords for your original songs.

THE TONIC CHORD

The tonic chord (I) is often the first—and almost always the last—chord in the song. I is most often preceded by V7, and the "next most likely" chord to precede I is the IV chord.

DIATONIC CHORDS AND SECONDARY DOMINANT CHORDS

Simple folk tunes, pop tunes, and blues often contain diatonic chords only. Therefore, if we are going to work out the chords to a simple melody in C, the chords with the highest probability of being played are the following: C, Dm, Em, F, G7 and Am (the Bm♭5 is seldom used in actual practice). The next "most likely" group of chords would be the secondary dominant chords:

C7, D7, E7, F7, A7, and B7.

OUR SONG MODEL: "MICHAEL"

We will use as our song model the popular folk tune, "Michael." Working phrase-by-phrase, we will learn to locate the proper chords by analyzing the melody. To keep things simple, our analysis deals mainly with diatonic chords. For ease of reference, each measure is numbered.

FIRST PHRASE

With the exception of the A note, all of the notes in the first phrase are either C, E, or G.

Principle: If most of the notes in a phrase belong to a particular chord, try that chord to see if it "sounds right."

Solution: The chord for this phrase is C (C-E-G).

94

SECOND PHRASE

The last two beats of the third measure could be a C chord, but it is more colorful to place I7 (C7) between I (C) and IV (F) when possible. The only time this is prohibited is when there is a major seventh tone (B) in the melody.

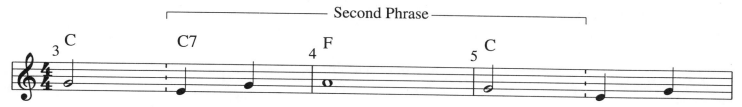

Principle: Try playing I7 between I and IV.

Any note that is carried for one-and-a-half beats or more (𝅘𝅥𝅭 in 4/4 time) is likely to be a tone in the accompanying chord. Therefore, the four-beat "A" note tells us that the accompanying chord "probably" has an "A" note in it. The first question is this: "What chords in C contain the A note?" Answer: Dm (D-F-A); F (F-A-C); and Am (A-C-E). After trying each of the chords, we decide the F sounds best.

Principles: A) Note duration can help identify chord tones.
              B) It is best to try several chords for each possible harmony.
              C) Try the appropriate diatonic chords first.
              D) Knowledge (theory) provides shortcuts.
              E) The ear is the final judge.

The G note at the end of phrase two is two beats. What chords in the key of C contain the G note? Answer: C (C-E-G); Em (E-G-B); Am (A-C-E). After trying them all, the C sounds the "best." The two notes beginning the third phrase (E and G) also support the case for the C chord in measure five. Finally, the plagal cadence (IV-I) is a typical change at the end of a phrase.

Principle: Look for familiar cadences (see Chapter Five) at the end of phrases.

THIRD PHRASE

Measure six begins with the notes G and E. These notes belong to both the C chord (C-E-G) and the iiim chord, Em (E-G-B). Either chord would work, but let's use Em for the nice change of mood it offers.

Principles: A) I and iiim are potentially interchangeable (tonic function).
              B) Using iiim instead of I often creates a fresh-sounding harmony.

The next three notes—F, E, and D—(measures 6-7) give us the opportunity to use a "diatonic chord passage" using the melody tones as the chord roots.

Principle: Sometimes a scalewise (note to note) series of tones can be harmonized with the
                 corresponding diatonic chords. In such cases, each note should have a time value
                 of at least one or more beats.

FOURTH (FINAL) PHRASE

No chord change is needed for the second half of measure seven. The two-beat E note at the beginning of measure eight is found in C (C-E-G), Em (E-G-B), and Am (A-C-E). C is the usual chord here (the C chord would fit into the diatonic descending chord sequence (F-Em-Dm-C). C is a good choice, but I am using Am (A-C-E) to provide a "reharmonized" sound, and to show you the vim *for* I *substitute*.

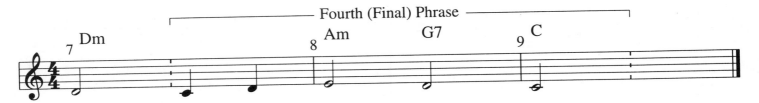

Principle: Substitute vim for I when it improves the overall sound.

Ending the final phrase is the perfect cadence, V7-I, which is G7-C in this key.

Michael (With Chords)

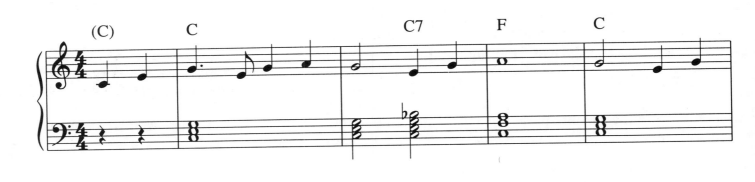

GUITAR CHORDS

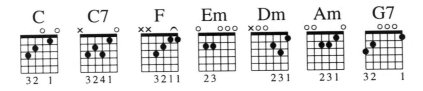

96

ADDITIONAL TIPS FOR MATCHING CHORDS TO MELODIES

1. To branch out beyond the use of diatonic chords only, work towards mastering the fundamental chord theory taught in Chapter Five.

2. Songs with fast tempos usually have fewer chords than songs with slow tempos.

3. The chords should create the appropriate emotion for the lyrics. Major triads are bright and happy. The lonesome sound of minor chords makes them the ideal match for sad lyrics. For tension that demands resolution, the dominant, diminished, and augmented chords are good choices.

4. Select the right chords for the style. Triads are often good for folk songs and simple country and rock songs. Seventh chords sound more sophisticated. Tunes associated with jazz and Broadway use a lot of "uptown" chords like ninths, thirteenths, and chords with altered (sharped or flatted) fifths and ninths.

ANALYZING AND LISTENING

Space limitations do not permit us to delve into other relationships between chords and melodies at this time. However, I believe the foregoing analysis of "Michael" can help the novice achieve a new way of thinking about chords; that is, know your theory, experiment, and learn to improve existing harmonies wherever possible.

The analytical methods taught here can help you find out "why" certain chords are used at certain times —all that is needed is to begin *analyzing and listening* on a regular basis. Applied chord theory can be an addicting hobby, and I hope the last two chapters have helped whet your appetite for more knowledge about this fascinating subject.

SUGGESTED PROJECTS

1. Add harmony to any basic melody in a beginner's violin or clarinet method book.
2. Analyzing the chords and melody of any song in sheet music, attempt to devise your own "rules" regarding the matching of chords to melody.
3. Test the following chord substitutions in any song of your own choice:

   A) iiim for I
   B) vim for I

Do these substitutions seem to improve the harmony in the context you have chosen?

7

RHYTHM

When people discuss "the beat" of a song, they are really talking about rhythm. From the steady two-beat bass of polkas and military marches to the freeform rhythms of modern jazz, "the beat" strongly influences each person's tendency to like or dislike a particular song or style.

In this chapter, we will study the most popular rhythms of contemporary music. Hopefully, these rhythm lessons will enable you to set your original music to "the beat" that best enhances its melody and lyrics.

4/4 TIME

Also known as *common time*, 4/4 is the most common time signature for popular music. The fundamental rhythm of 4/4 is 4 quarter notes to the measure. Songs in 4/4 may be played with either a *straight time* or a *sixteenth-note* feel.

4/4 STRAIGHT TIME

In *straight time*, the beat is divided into two equal parts. This gives a four-beat measure the even feeling of ONE and TWO and THREE and FOUR and. The following examples are typical straight-time rhythms:

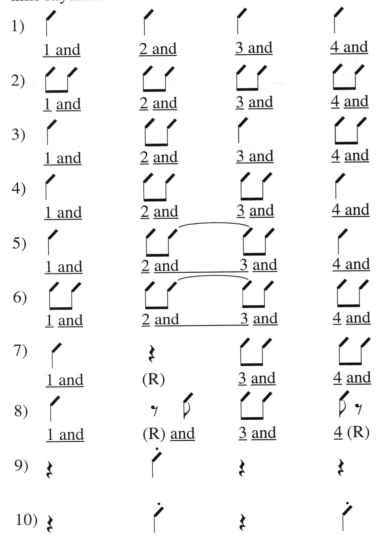

(R) = Rest

Apply any chord (or chord progression) of your own choice to these straight-time rhythms. For best results, listen closely to the instrumentation on a number of straight-time recordings.

Placing an accent on the even-numbered downbeats (two and four) creates the *backbeat*, a simple accenting pattern associated with rock, R&B, and some country and jazz styles.

Examples of straight-time songs: "Johnny B. Goode," "Margaritaville," "Yesterday," and "Wonderful Tonight."

4/4 WITH A SIXTEENTH-NOTE FEEL

Funk, reggae, rap, and some rock and soul tunes are played in *4/4 with a sixteenth-note feel*. The sixteenth-note "groove" divides each beat into four equal parts, and there is often an emphasis on *syncopation:* the accenting of upbeats. Check out some recordings by the Watts 103rd Street Rhythm Band, Kool and the Gang, and James Brown to hear some great funk sounds.

Here are some typical sixteenth-note rhythms, beginning with the most basic:

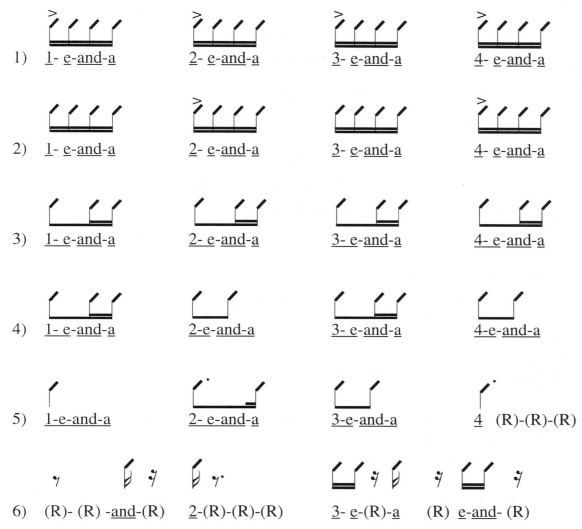

Sometimes a four-syllable word is used to count sixteenth notes; i.e., MIS-SIS-SIP-PI; CAT-ER-PIL-LAR; etc. In the above examples, the fractions of the beat enclosed in parentheses are rests. Examples of 4/4 *sixteenth-note* songs: "Slipping into Darkness," "I Shot the Sheriff," and "Down and Out in New York City."

TRIPLET FEEL

When the beat is divided into three equal parts, the music is said to have a *triplet feel*. This rhythm can often be identified by listening for the triplets played on the cymbal by the drummer. Triplet-feel songs are usually played at slow to moderate tempos; the slower songs are sometimes called *ballads*. Technically, songs with a triplet feel should be notated in *compound time;* that is, 6/8, 9/8, 12/8, etc.

The fundamental 12/8 triplet rhythm is:

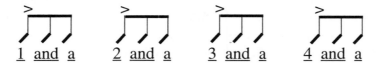

It is not necessary to place a 3 above the groups of eighth-note triplets in compound time.

Table 9: Basic note values in 12/8 time

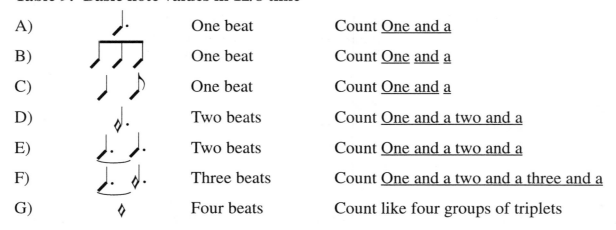

A)		One beat	Count <u>One and a</u>
B)		One beat	Count <u>One and a</u>
C)		One beat	Count <u>One and a</u>
D)		Two beats	Count <u>One and a two and a</u>
E)		Two beats	Count <u>One and a two and a</u>
F)		Three beats	Count <u>One and a two and a three and a</u>
G)		Four beats	Count like four groups of triplets

Example C (above) is a *shuffle triplet*; this time figure is explained on the next page.

In 12/8 time, the eighth note ♪ receives one-third of a beat, and the quarter note ♩ receives two-thirds of a beat. Here are some more 12/8 rhythms:

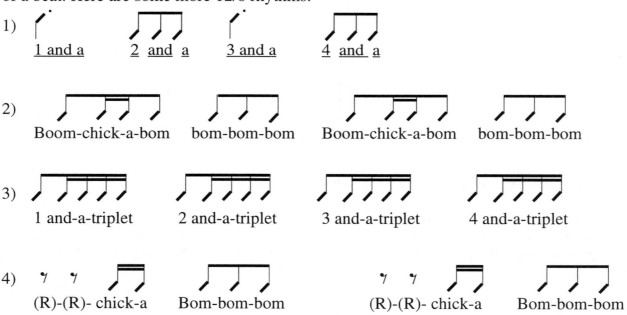

Example C may be counted "bom chick-a chick-a." Listen to some '50s vocal group music and you will get a good feel for these rhythms. Caution:12/8 songs are often written in 4/4 to simplify the notation. 12/8 country tunes are quite frequently notated in "cut time" (p. 105) to emphasize the two-beat bass pattern, and 9/8 country waltzes are usually written in 3/4.

Examples of "12/8 triplet" songs: "End of the World," "Earth Angel," "This Boy," "True Blue," "Funny How Time Slips Away," "Make The World Go Away," and "Color My World."

12/8 SHUFFLE

The *12/8 shuffle* beat is used in all popular styles, but it is most closely associated with the blues. Here is the basic 12/8 shuffle:

The same rhythm is also written in either of the following styles:

A)   B)   shuffle

Example B is indicated at the beginning of songs that are written in straight time, but interpreted in shuffle time. The shuffle rhythm may also have a rest in the middle. This rhythm may be written in either of the following styles:

A)   B)

A typical method of playing the shuffle rhythm is to alternate between the fifth and sixth of the chord, using the chord root as a drone:

Typical Shuffle Rhythm

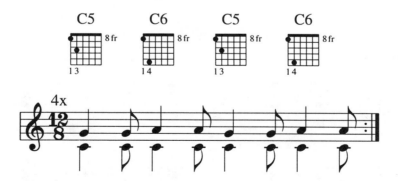

The shuffle triplet is known by various names, including: *swing eighths*, *jazz eighths*, and *lazy eighths*.

The rhythm ♪♫ is sometimes used to indicate the shuffle beat. If your musical background is primarily classical, you should listen closely to some blues recordings to get a feel for the shuffle beat. Muddy Waters, Howlin' Wolf, and Elmore James are recommended artists.

Examples of rock and blues songs with a 12/8 shuffle beat: "Hootchie Koochie Man," "Blues with a Feeling," "Heartbreak Hotel," and "Stray Cat Strut." "I Fall to Pieces," and "Hello Walls" are "country shuffles."

3/4 TIME

3/4 time—also known as *waltz time*—is a mainstay of country music, and is not used as often in the other popular styles. The basic three-beat pattern starts with the chord root, followed by two quarter-note strums (ex. 1). When one chord is played for two measures in a row starting with an odd-numbered measure (1, 3, 5, etc.), the *alternating bass* pattern is used (ex. 2).

3/4 Country Style

GUITAR CHORDS

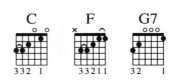

Country waltzes are often played to a shuffle beat or a triplet feel, making the true time signature 9/8. Played with a lilting sound, waltzes are popular for slow dancing, and instrumentation is kept to a minimum. 3/4 tunes in rock music are usually played in straight-time.

Songs in 3/4 time: "Tennessee Waltz," "Almost Persuaded," "Could I Have This Dance," "Michelle," "Time in a Bottle," and "Annie's Song."

"CUT" TIME

The symbol for *"cut" time* is ¢. Cut-time is a two-beat rhythm found in many styles including marches, polkas, ragtime, early New Orleans, jazz, bluegrass, folk-dance music, rock, and country. The reason we count "in two" is because cut-time tunes are performed too fast to conveniently tap four-to-the-bar. The cut-time feel is sometimes accomplished by a *root-fifth* bass pattern accompanied by chords on the upbeat:

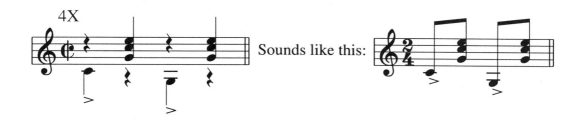

Cut-time tunes are often transcribed in 4/4 for ease of reading. Consequently, it is important to listen to a recording to acquire the correct sense of a song's meter. Many songs may be performed in either cut-time *or* common time, according to the interpretation of the artist.

Songs in cut time: "Good Hearted Woman," "Hey, Good Lookin'," "Jambalaya," "Beer Barrel Polka," and "The Entertainer."

SUGGESTED PROJECTS

1. Using recordings of your own choice, find a song in each of the following rhythms:

   A) 4/4 straight time
   B) 4/4 with a sixteenth-note feel
   C) 12/8 triplet feel
   D) 12/8 shuffle
   E) 3/4 time
   F) 9/8 "country waltz"
   G) "Cut" time (two-beat)

2. Locate a 12/8 song that has been notated (in sheet music) in 4/4.

3. Locate a 9/8 song that has been notated in 3/4.

8

COPYRIGHT AND LEAD SHEETS

We conclude our songwriting study with some fundamental information about copyright procedures and lead sheets. All songwriters should be acquainted with the basics of copyright law. Without copyright protection, artistic persons would have great difficulty maintaining control over their original works. Here, you will learn how to register your original songs with the Copyright Office in Washington, D.C.

The lead sheet is a basic sketch of a song in notation form. Lead sheets can be used for various purposes: preservation of information, copyright, and efficient communication with other musicians. Upon completion of this chapter, you should be able to prepare lead sheets with no problem.

COPYRIGHT

A *copyright* is a legally granted right to ownership of a literary, musical, or artistic work. Your original song is protected by copyright law from the moment it is first written down or recorded. The copyright law defines writing down or recording the song as *fixed form*.

Place the symbol © on your song to give notice that you are claiming authorship. Write down the year the music was created and include your name after the symbol. If there are any collaborators, include their names as well. If a copyright is owned by a publishing company, the company name will follow the date (see the first page of this book for an example).

COPYRIGHT REGISTRATION

If you wish, you may register your copyright with the Copyright Office:

Register of Copyrights
Library of Congress
Washington, D.C. 20559
(202) 287-8700

To apply for registration, write (or call) the copyright office and ask for form PA. Complete the registration form (instructions are included), then mail it back with a filing fee of $20 per song *and* a tape or lead sheet of each song. If you decide to send a recording (cassette tape), you do not have to include written music, and the recording does not need to be fancy. If you do not wish to send a recording, a simple lead sheet is fine. After several weeks, you will receive a certificate bearing the Copyright Office seal, and your copyright will be officially registered.

ADVANTAGES OF REGISTERING YOUR COPYRIGHT

Although copyright registration is not required, copyright holders do acquire valuable legal benefits that make registration worthwhile. First, there is documentation of the date of creation and authorship. In addition, a Copyright Office registration gives you access to statutory damages ($200 to $100,000 maximum) for infringement.

MORE THAN ONE SONG?

It is permissible to register several songs as a collection and still pay only $20 per application. Simply give your collection of songs a title, fill out form PA, and return the form with the fee to the Copyright Office. Be sure to include a tape or lead sheet for each song in the collection. If you are sending a taped collection, all of the songs may be on one tape.

The potential inconvenience of registering unpublished songs as a collection is this: If you should later sell an individual song from the collection, you will have to be sure that the copyright transfer does not give the buyer all of the other songs, too. In other words, you might need to hire a copyright attorney to read the fine print. In such cases, you may need to apply for a new registration of the song that you are selling, and tell the Copyright Office why you are seeking the new registration. All of these potential problems can be avoided by registering one song at a time in the first place.

AUTHENTICITY IS THE RESPONSIBILITY OF THE CLAIMANT

Always be sure the work you are registering is original before sending it to the Copyright Office. Their job is not to check for – or verify – authenticity. The copyright registration is merely a verification that you have *claimed* original ownership on a certain date.

LENGTH OF COPYRIGHT PROTECTION

The 1978 copyright law extends copyright protection for the life of the author *plus* 50 years. Previous laws required renewals at 28-year intervals, and copyright protection would sometimes lapse within an author's lifetime.

LEAD SHEETS

A *lead sheet* is a basic outline of a song's lyrics, melody and chords. Lead sheets are normally written in the treble clef. Here is a lead sheet for "Frankie and Johnnie":

Frankie And Johnnie

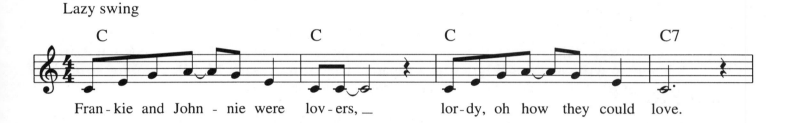

TIPS FOR LEAD SHEETS

1. Place the song title at the top center of the first page.

2. Draw all notes, symbols and lyrics as clearly as possible.

3. Describe the tempo or mood of the song with terms like "swing," "lively," "moderate," etc. Place this description at the top left of the music. It often helps to include a precise metronome marking such as $\quarternote = 84$.

4. Notate your lead sheet in the treble clef, and be sure to include the key signature and the time signature.

5. Lyrics may be capitalized for ease of reading.

6. Vocal slurs (one word that falls on two or more different pitches) should be connected with a dash (John-nie, mes. 1), or followed with a line (done___, mes. 10).

7. Draw a line after a word that is held on one pitch through a tie (man —, mes. 9-10).

8. Label section parts for songs that have two or more sections (verse/chorus; A - A - B - A; etc.).

9. Space permitting, extra lyrics may be written below the initial lyrics. Or, simply write the additional lyrics at the bottom of the lead sheet, taking care to label sections as needed. It is also acceptable to write additional lyrics on a separate page if necessary. Mel Bay's *Song Writer's Manuscript Book*, with only six staves per page, is ideal for lyricists.

10. Keep the chord symbols accurate but simple. If necessary, a good arranger can develop the harmonies later.

11. Include the copyright notice at the bottom of the sheet.

12. A great way to study the layout of lead sheets is to analyze the music in any *fake book*. A fake book is a large collection of lead sheets in a songbook.

PURPOSE OF THE LEAD SHEET

It is not necessary to submit a lead sheet to the Copyright Office to register a copyright (a tape will do), but it is handy to have a lead sheet for rehearsals and recording. The lead sheet, while not a full arrangement, serves as a basic "roadmap" for musicians to follow in rehearsals and studio situations; thus, time and money are saved while greater musical accuracy is assured. Of course, elaborate recordings may require the services of a music *arranger*. The arranger develops specific instrumental and vocal parts from the lead sheet.

GLOSSARY

BLUES – A style of music created by Southern blacks in the late 1800s. The predominant blues form is a 12-bar chord progression with three 4-bar vocal phrases, harmonized with the I7, IV7, and V7 chords.

BRIDGE – The bridge is a song section that is different from the verse, chorus, or main section or theme. Used most prominently as the B section of AABA tunes, the bridge can also be a third section of a verse-chorus song. Unlike a chorus, the bridge serves as a "link" that connects the other sections together.

CHORUS – 1) A self-contained song section that functions as a contrast to the verse. The chorus usually contains the same lyrics each time through. 2) To a musician, a "chorus" refers to the entire chord progression (played once) of any tune (32-bar AABA, 12-bar blues, etc.).

CODA – A brief section at the close of a song which often includes several repetitions of the song hook or title.

EXTENSION – Often called a coda, the extension is a short lyrical section sung at the end of a tune for the first time (listen to "By the Time I Get to Phoenix").

FORM – The format or structure of a composition. In popular music, the most common forms are known as AAA, AABA, verse/chorus, and The Blues.

HOOK – 1) A lyric that is intended to "catch" and hold the listener's attention. Usually sung repeatedly, the lyrical hook is often the title of the song. 2) A memorable instrumental riff or phrase, also designed to catch the attention of the listener ("Pretty Woman" guitar intro).

INSTRUMENTAL BREAK – Also known as the solo, the instrumental break helps to provide contrast to the singing. Usually played over the chord changes of one (or more) of the song's sections, the instrumental break may be either extemporaneous or pre-arranged.

INTERLUDE – Sometimes called an instrumental bridge, the interlude is a relatively brief instrumental section, often played to chords not found in the main section(s). The interlude connects one section to another (often with a dramatic flourish) while providing variety.

INTRODUCTION – A section of music that precedes the main body of the song, the introduction or "intro" is usually instrumental, but some intros are spoken, hummed, or whistled.

MELODY – A succession of tones that conveys a musical idea; often known as the "tune" to the listener.

MODULATION – A change of key that occurs during the performance of a song.

OUTRO – An instrumental coda or ending.

POPULAR MUSIC – Also known as commercial music, Top 40, etc., popular music is the mass-produced music, featured at concerts and on the radio, performed by popular entertainers, that is commercially marketed to the general public.

REFRAIN – The repeating lyrical section at the end of the verses in the AAA *with refrain* song form (Chapter Two).

TRANSPOSE – To change the key of a song, often for the purpose of accommodating a vocalist or instrumentalist.

VERSE – A song section that uses the same melody with different lyrics each time. Found in the AAA, AAA with refrain, and verse/chorus song forms (see Chapter Two).

ESSENTIAL SUPPLIES FOR NEW SONG WRITERS

Some song writers work with only pencil and paper, others use only a tape recorder, and many have fully equipped home studios with professional notation equipment. In most cases, the following supplies will be all you need to get started.

1. A good rhyming dictionary

2. A thesaurus

3. An up-to-date dictionary

4. Extra PA copyright forms

5. A small tape recorder

6. Manuscript paper

7. For guitarists and keyboard players, a good chord encyclopedia:

   a) *Mel Bay's Deluxe Encyclopedia of Guitar Chords*

   b) *Mel Bay's Deluxe Encyclopedia of Piano Chords*

8. A current copy of *Song Writer's Market* (published annually)

   Song Writer's Market is an essential book which lists over 2,500 industry contacts including publishers, record companies, song writer's organizations, performing rights associations, managers, and much more. Indispensable for anyone who is interested in commercial writing. Available from:

   > Writer's Digest Book
   > 1507 Dana Avenue
   > Cincinnati, Ohio 45207

9. The following Mel Bay Publications books contain an abundance of information concerning music theory, composers, and composing:

   a) *Theory and Harmony for Everyone*

   b) *You Can Teach Yourself About Music*

   c) *Student's Guide to the Great Composers*

   d) *Basic Concepts of Arranging and Orchestrating Music*

   e) *The Lawless New Theory Series* (three workbooks and an answers book)

50 CHORDS FOR KEYBOARD

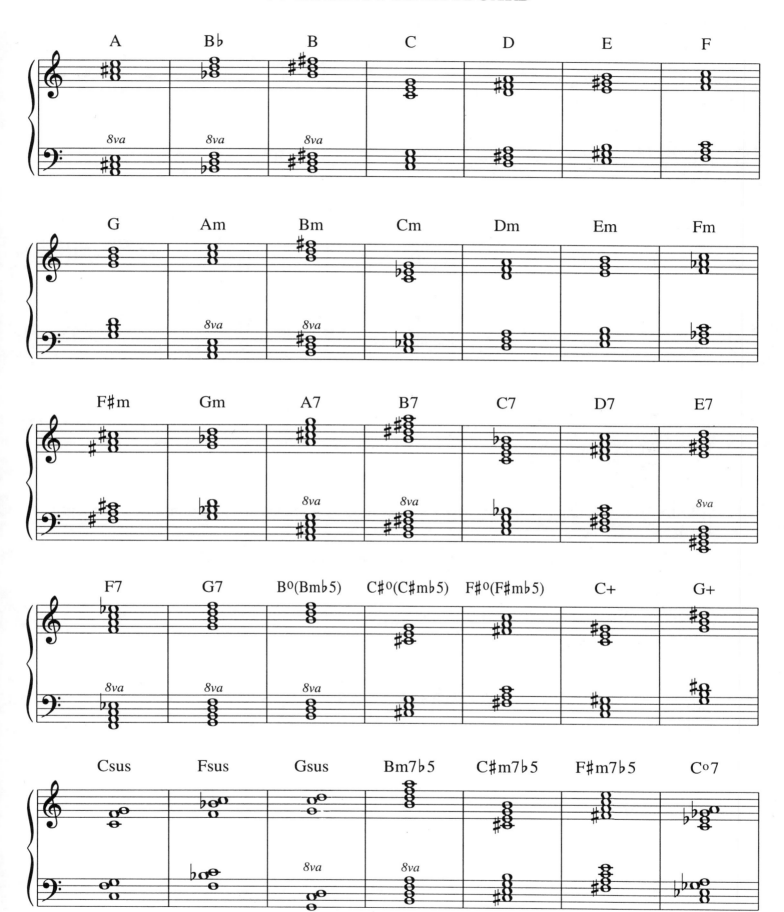

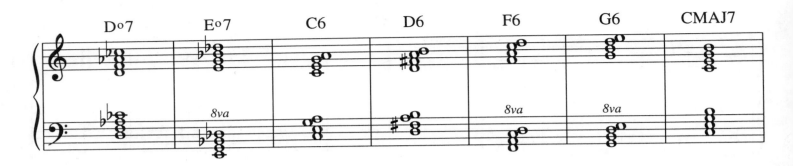

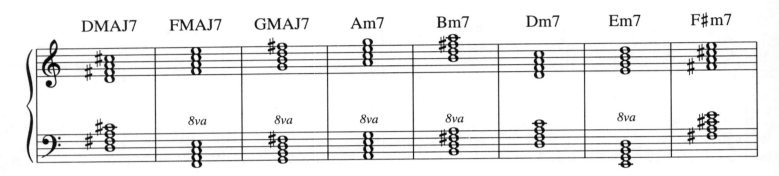

NOTES ON KEYBOARD CHORDS

1. Because of the fundamental nature of this book, most of the keyboard voicings are in root position in the musical examples throughout the text.

2. The songs in Chapter Five are ideal for teaching beginners the basic root-position chords. Instructors are encouraged to use these songs as models for teaching inversions and basic voice-leading.

3. For more keyboard chords, refer to **Mel Bay's Deluxe Encyclopedia of Piano Chords.**

50 CHORDS FOR THE GUITAR

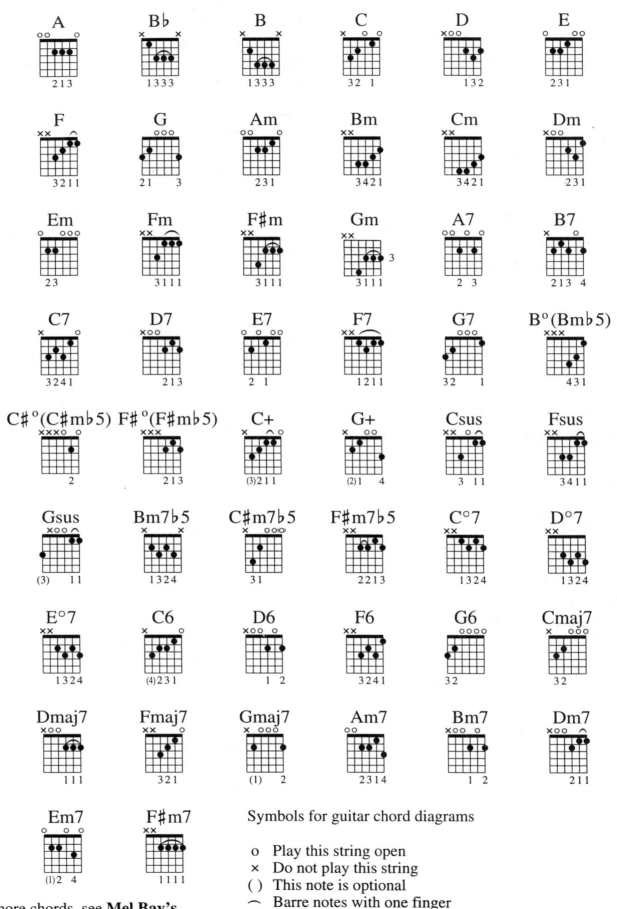

Symbols for guitar chord diagrams

o   Play this string open
×   Do not play this string
( ) This note is optional
⌒ Barre notes with one finger

For more chords, see **Mel Bay's
Deluxe Encyclopedia of Guitar Chords.**

INDEX OF RECORDED EXAMPLES

YOU CAN TEACH YOURSELF
SONG WRITING—ON TAPE!

A companion cassette recording to *You Can Teach Yourself Song Writing* is available by contacting your local music dealer, or you may order direct from:

Mel Bay Publications
#4 Industrial Drive
Dailey Industrial Park
Pacific, MO 63069

1-800-8-MEL BAY

• Cassette contains all musical examples listed in Index of Recorded Music (see previous page).

• Hearing the music will help you learn faster and more efficiently.

• Playing along with the taped piano and guitar parts insures accuracy of interpretation.

• Tape costs less than one private lesson!

TITLE

COMPOSER(S)

TITLE

COMPOSER(S)

TITLE

COMPOSER(S)

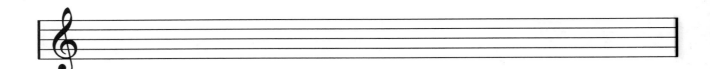